MORAL FREEDOM

JEFFREY OLEN

Temple University Press
Philadelphia

Temple University Press, Philadelphia 19122

Copyright © 1988 by Temple University. All rights reserved

Published 1988

Printed in the United States of America

The paper used in this publication meets the minimum requirements of American National Standard for Information Sciences—Permanence of Paper for Printed Library Materials, ANSI Z39.48-1984

LIBRARY OF CONGRESS

Library of Congress Cataloging-in-Publication Data

Olen, Jeffrey.
  Moral freedom / Jeffrey Olen.
    p. cm.
  Includes index.
  ISBN 0-87722-578-8
  1. Free will and determinism. I. Title.
BJ1461.039 1988
170—dc19   88-15916
                                                              CIP

For John Atwell

CONTENTS

PREFACE

BACK WHEN I WAS A GRADUATE STUDENT, the first member of the philosophy faculty to befriend me was John Atwell. In his office and in bars and pool halls, we talked about life and death, sex and love, ethics and philosophy--sometimes seriously, sometimes in the casual, bantering way that usually accompanies Scotch or beer. Nietzsche, whose work I'd started reading long before I took my first philosophy course, was as much a staple as the pretzel.

My professional interest in ethics and Nietzsche waned during my trek toward the doctorate, and I ended up writing my dissertation in epistemology. Atwell sneeringly but good-naturedly called it my "S knows that p dissertation," and even though he fully appreciated my reasons for moving in that direction, every now and then he reminded me not to forget the concerns that first got me interested in philosophy.

I went on to write other things after graduate school, but nothing in ethics until the obligatory chapters of an introductory text. Atwell criticized one of those chapters extensively, but along with Elizabeth Beardsley he was bold enough to ask me to write a volume for a series in occupational ethics they were editing. I was rash enough to accept.

Then Jane Cullen, my editor for the intro text, moved to Temple University Press. I was among her former authors she called to sound out about new projects. My first thought was to write a long-planned book in philosophy of science. My second was to reflect on what I'd written in ethics and on Atwell's periodic reminders.

This time I'd write a book in ethics that reflected the concerns that first got me interested in philosophy.

That's why this book is dedicated to John Atwell.

IT MIGHT ALSO HAVE BEEN DEDICATED to Jane Cullen, who remained as encouraging and supportive as ever through the writing of what no doubt turned out to be an odder book than she'd bargained for.

One thing that makes it odd is its style. I wrote it in my own voice--all my voices, rather, including my irreverent voice, my impatient voice, my professional voice, and, toward the end, my meditative voice. The decision to do that was deliberate, though somewhat after the fact. In the beginning I simply wrote, as naturally as I knew how. Only later did I decide to leave the voices undisturbed.

Two things led to that decision. First, there was the genuine pleasure I was experiencing in writing the book. The issues, the arguments, and the words were all deeply felt. They engaged me personally as well as intellectually, and the natural thing to do was write that way. It was also the enjoyable thing to do, and I didn't want the enjoyment to end.

Second, there was the theme of the book. *Moral Freedom* is, among other things, about the claims of what I call the *personal* moral point of view against what is often called *the* moral point of view but I call the *impersonal* moral point of view. It seemed perfectly fitting, then, that I write it in a personal, not impersonal, voice--mine. To put it another way, I could no more write it in the style of the neo-Kantians (my main foils) than Nietzsche could write in the style of Kant (his main foil). The book is quite Nietzschean in spirit that way, and I thank Jane for putting up with it. (After the Press's board approved my proposal, Jane told me that one member expressed the hope that the Preface would explain why I treat some very important matters so facetiously. I trust that it just did.)

Here's another thing that makes it odd: It kept changing on me, much the way a novel keeps changing on its author. The reason is that I began it with many issues still unsettled. That made the book a learning experience for me. It also gave some sections a certain let's-try-this-no-that-doesn't-work-let's-try-that flavor, as one reviewer of the proposal put it. In redrafting individual chapters, I softened that flavor a bit, but I didn't eliminate it. I like books that record the author's explorations instead of merely reporting their results. I thank Jane for putting up with that, too.

And I thank John Vollrath for pointing out places where the book could be more judicious, and Jean Rumsey for being such a good sounding board for my thoughts on Kant, and Carolee Cote for all her wizardry on the word processor, and UWSP for the sabbatical leave during which I completed this book, and Corinne Olen for-- oh, for all sorts of things. I also thank James Sterba for sparking the book's final reflections, and Joseph Margolis for more comments than I could possibly deal with to his satisfaction, and Doris Braendel for being a writer's dream of a copy editor.

And, of course, John Atwell--not just for our early conversations and the periodic reminders, but also for our more recent conversations on ethics and practical reason. We disagree on much, but without his influence this would have been a very different book.

J. O.
Stevens Point, WI
October, 1987

MORAL FREEDOM

1

TRUISMS

MORAL RULES ARE SOCIETY'S RULES. Many people take that to be a truism. Then again, many people—many of the same people, in fact—take this to be a truism: Morality is a matter of individual choice. Then again, many people—and again, many of the same people—take this to be a truism: Some things, deliberate cruelty for kicks, for example—are wrong regardless of what any society or individual has to say about them.

Philosophers who like to uncover contradictions can have a field day with these three truisms. So, for that matter, can philosophers who like to uncover—or, perhaps, create—ambiguities in order to resolve apparent contradictions. Others are more inclined to accept one truism and boldly dismiss the other two.

I am strongly inclined to accept all three. Whether a consistent and plausible moral theory can incorporate them remains to be seen. But I am convinced that any plausible moral theory must incorporate something *like* them. At the very minimum, it must allow the following weakened versions of them.

First, moral rules arise as social conventions and are maintained as social conventions, and these rules are, to varying degrees, morally binding on the members of that society.

Second, these rules leave the members of that society a generous degree of moral freedom. That is, there are many morally significant situations in which no single decision is required by these rules.

Third, society's rules and individual decisions may be seriously defective.

Once again, these are weakened versions of our three truisms. They are also (deliberately) vague. Depending on how someone chooses to interpret them, they can be so weak as to be utterly trivial, as strong as the original truisms, or anyplace in between. The purpose of this book is to find the correct interpretations.

LET'S TAKE A LOOK AT THE FIRST. One way of expressing its point is this. Moral rules are the product of a social contract. That is, they are mutually agreed upon rules among the members of a given society.

That there is a social contract is a commonplace, generally voiced by editorial writers and the like when the contract seems in danger of breaking down—when large numbers of teenagers no longer agree that it is wrong to shake people down on the subway, for instance, and when others no longer agree that preemptive strikes against suspected would-be muggers are wrong. That violators will always be with us shows that the social contract is not a matter of unanimous agreement. But the fear we experience when we no longer feel safe in subways, on the streets or in our own homes shows how much we rely on large-scale, if less than unanimous, agreement.

The agreement is, of course, a tacit one. None of us formally agrees to abide by the rules of society. Rather, we learn that other people will expect us to obey them and that we can expect others to obey them as well. At the same time, we learn to behave accordingly. It is this combination of mutual expectation and corresponding appropriate behavior that constitutes the social contract.

Of course, not all shared expectations and behaviors are part of our morality. Excluded are rules of etiquette, for example, and such other generally shared behaviors as watching the Super Bowl.

What, precisely, belongs to the social contract that constitutes our shared morality? That is a more controversial question than many people seem to realize, so I won't try to give a final answer until later. For now, I will borrow an answer from Kurt Baier, which gives the bare minimum[1]. Moral rules are the mutually agreed upon rules intended to provide reasons for acting that override reasons of self-interest when the interests of individuals conflict. (Baier prefers "whenever," but that may be too strong.) Included are rules against lying, promise-breaking, theft, cheating, and the like, as well as those against various forms of physical violence.

The stipulation that moral rules are intended to provide overriding reasons for acting should not be misunderstood. For one thing, it does not say that moral reasons *are* overriding. Whether they are is a matter of some controversy. Nor does it say that they are intended *always* to be overriding. That, too, is a matter of some controversy. It is enough that they are intended to be overriding in most cases.

That they are so intended is a practical point, not a conceptual or definitional one. Society requires cooperation, and cooperation requires trust. And morality provides the basis of that trust. If moral reasons did not override reasons of self-interest in most cases, individuals could have no assurance that their trust was well placed. The reasonable expectation would be that others will act on reasons of self-interest, not of morality. In that case we would be stuck with one of two kinds of society—either something like Central Park at night, which hardly counts as society at all, or something like the society envisioned by Hobbes and Orwell, which makes individuals so frightened of the consequences of breaking the rules that they believe it is always in their interest to follow them.

It is a good thing, then, that most of us generally *take* moral reasons to be overriding, whether they are or are not. That is, it is a good thing that we often act on them when it is not in our interest to do so, even if reason does not require that we do.

THE ABOVE SKETCH OMITS much of importance. In particular, it leaves out our second and third truisms. Consider the second. Morality is a matter of individual choice.

If we accept that, then we must also accept this. The social contract has no moral authority over any individual. Individuals are morally free to refuse to sign on, to leave, and to reject or accept any part of the social contract. If an individual does choose to join, it is the fact of his decision that makes society's rules morally binding on him. Without that decision, they are not morally binding on him. And even with it, if he changes his mind, they are no longer morally binding on him. He may be judged to act immorally according to society's rules, but that judgment has no greater moral force than the judgment that he acts immorally according to the code of Hammurabi. According to his own light, he does not act immorally, and because morality is a matter of individual choice, that is all that is morally important.

This is not to say that these choices can be made capriciously. There is, after all, a difference between acting morally and doing whatever strikes one's fancy. What that difference might be on this view is a question I'll have to return to.

According to this way of looking at things, then, even though moral rules arise and are maintained by social agreement, that agreement has no monopoly on morality. In addition to shared rules, morality includes individual codes of behavior, personal moral codes. Moreover, these personal moral codes are morally fundamental. Society's rules morally bind individuals only if individuals incorporate them into their personal codes. And individuals are immoral only if they have no such codes or don't keep faith with them. Whether they join the social contract is irrelevant.

To say the above is to deny that moral rules provide overriding reasons for acting for all members of society. Indeed, it may be to deny that they provide any reasons for acting whatever for some members of society.

The argument goes like this. Someone has a reason for acting only if a proposed reason fits into her network of desires, goals, and personal projects—only, that is, if it is capable of motivating her. If a moral rule does not advance her desires, goals or personal projects, it does not provide any reasons for *her* to act. That is why the mutually agreed upon rules of other individuals are not morally binding on her. A moral rule morally binds someone only if it provides her with a reason for acting.

And even if it does provide her with a reason for acting, it may not provide her with an overriding one. Most of us, after all, do share certain attitudes toward others—sympathy, concern, and respect. Because we do, moral rules do provide us with reasons for acting. But whether they override other reasons in particular cases must be a matter of personal decision. My own projects also provide reasons for acting, and my personal moral code may give them more weight than the reasons provided by rules that I accept. Just as my desires, goals, and projects determine what may be reasons for me to act, so do they determine the relative weight of those reasons.

Truisms

WHAT I HAVE JUST OFFERED is a view of morality that allows individuals an extremely generous degree of moral freedom, one that refuses to weaken our second truism. Where does that leave the first? Pretty well intact, I think. It does not deny that moral rules are social conventions. It merely adds that there is more to morality than moral rules. Is it plausible?

Here's one point in its favor. It seems to capture the way many ordinary people—nonphilosophers, that is—think about morality and, I suspect, the way many philosophers treat morality when they are not philosophizing. Many people do lie and break promises—not only because some other moral rule takes precedence but also because some personal project takes precedence. Sometimes they will agree that they acted wrongly in doing so, but at other times they will not. And they are willing to make precisely the same judgments when others break promises to them under similar circumstances.

That, however, is only one point in its favor. Its plausibility must rest on much more. Is the distinction between moral rules and a personal moral code a legitimate one? That is something I'll explore later. Something else I'll explore later is this: Is it true that a reason for acting can be a reason for some particular individual to act only if it is capable of motivating her? Or, to put the question in the way that many moral philosophers, following Bernard Williams, put it, is it true that people can have only internal reasons for acting, and not external reasons as well?[2] If that is not true, our second truism must be weakened, perhaps considerably.

Here's why. If moral rules provide reasons for acting, then—on the assumption that people can have external reasons for acting—they provide reasons for acting for all members of a particular society, regardless of their desires, goals, and projects. In that case, the rules are morally binding for all members, regardless of their decisions to sign on. As Baier would have it, morality is not the sort of thing we volunteer for.[3] Moreover, if the reasons provided by moral rules are better reasons than reasons of self-interest, then they provide overriding reasons for all members of society, regardless of the ease with which many of us lie or break promises to further our own projects.

Although this view of morality—the externalist view, we can call it—is more restrictive of individual moral freedom than the other— the internalist view—it still leaves members of society a generous degree of moral freedom. There remain many morally significant situations in which no single decision is required by moral rules. That, of course, is the weakened version of our second truism.

One way the externalist view allows it is this. Moral rules often conflict, and when they do, there is not always a clearly discernible answer to the question, Which shall I follow? When there isn't, there is no Supreme Court of morality to settle the issue. The individual must decide for himself. Others may disagree with his decision, and they may judge it wrong by their own lights, but according to his own light he acted morally, and that is what is morally important.

Another way is this: Many morally significant situations are those in which questions of ultimate value, the good life, the sorts of personal projects we ought to pursue, arise. Although we are not morally free to choose any conception of the good life—being the best Mafia hit man in North America, for instance—we are not morally required to choose any particular one. As long as we do not make our choices in defiance of any overriding reasons, we are free to make them as we see best. Personal codes are not morally prior to moral rules, but they are not dictated by them.

Also, the externalist view can allow that the reasons provided by moral rules need not always be overriding. Indeed, it might be forced to allow it. Once again, people sometimes do break promises to pursue their personal projects, and most of us agree that they are not always wrong for doing it. That seems to be another way of saying that it is part of the social contract that reasons provided by moral rules are not always overriding. If it is, we are morally free to release ourselves from at least some of our obligations to pursue at least some of our projects. The extent of that moral freedom is something I'll return to later.

THE PLAUSIBILITY of the internalist view of morality—and, for that matter, the externalist view—depends on something else as well: our third truism. Some things are wrong regardless of what any society or individual has to say about them.

If we accept the third truism, we must also accept this: In some areas, the social contract has limited moral authority. There is some higher moral authority—not the individual—that morally supersedes it. We must also accept that there are moral limits to any individual's conception of the good life, that there is some higher moral authority—not just moral rules—that morally supersedes personal moral codes. What the third truism says, then, is that there are limits to the moral freedom of individuals acting collectively—they are not morally free to adopt some moral rules—and individually— they are not morally free to pursue some personal projects, nor are they morally free to pursue the rest in certain ways.

Numerous candidates for this higher authority have been nominated throughout the ages. God, of course, is one. A constellation of natural rights—life and liberty being the most prominent—is another. So is a moral law discoverable by reason. So is common sense.

This last one is, I think, particularly important, if only because it encapsulates a fourth truism—that morality is merely a matter of common sense. And that one, like the others, is one I'm strongly inclined to accept, if we strike out the "merely." That is why I claimed that any plausible moral theory must, at the very minimum, allow that some of society's rules and some individual decisions may be seriously defective—because they violate common sense. The sort of common sense I have in mind includes such things as consistency and ordinary means-ends reasoning.

Might society's rules and individual decisions also violate the will of God? Someone's natural rights? A moral law discoverable by reason?

I don't expect to have anything to say about the will of God in the rest of this book. Nor do I expect to have anything to say about natural rights, which, I suspect, can be made sense of only insofar as they follow from something like a moral law. But that last candidate—a moral law discoverable by reason—is one worth pursuing, at least in a demystified version. Can reason deliver moral— as well as commonsensical—constraints on the moral freedom of individuals and society? Can moral rules and individual decisions be seriously defective because they violate something other than common sense?

Kant certainly thought so, and his various statements of the categorical imperative tell us what they can violate and how. Neo-Kantians, like Baier, also think so. So, although in a much different way, did Aristotle. So, of course, did many other philosophers about whom I'll have much less to say.

SUPPOSE THAT SOMETHING like what they thought is correct. Where does that leave the first two truisms? The first can remain thoroughly intact. We can still say that moral rules are society's rules, but we will have to distinguish valid rules from invalid rules. We will also have to say that what makes them invalid is something other than a moral rule—some prerequisite that any valid rule must meet. What might that be? One possibility is a formal constraint conceptually linked to moral notions—which is one way of interpreting the categorical imperative. Another is a substantive constraint that can be shown, by some kind of transcendental argument, to be presupposed by the social contract. That is another way of interpreting the categorical imperative.

The second truism, however, will have to be weakened, but I'm not sure how much. Clearly, if the constraints are Kantian, individuals will not be morally permitted to pursue certain projects or to pursue others in certain ways. But if they are Aristotelian, then I'm not sure that the word "constraints" applies at all. Someone may have a seriously defective notion of the good life according to Aristotelian reasoning, but it does not follow by that same reasoning that she ought to change her ways.

Suppose we can rank conceptions of the good life as better or worse. Presumably, the conception of someone whose motto is "Eat, drink, and be merry for tomorrow we shall eat, drink, and be merry" will not rank very high. But if she has no interest in Goethe, Mozart, or Vermeer, and quiet contemplation is completely beyond her temperament, the claim that she has no reason to change her ways, much less an overriding one, is hard to dispute. Aristotelian reasoning may generate rankings, but it's hard to see how it can generate obligations. Cuts of meat can be ranked, but someone who likes her steak tough and tasteless has no reason to trade in her chuck for a prime strip.

I'll have more to say about all this later, but if it's right, it shows that the existence of better moralities need not interfere with an individual's moral freedom. And that suggests an interesting way of weakening the third truism. Instead of saying that some things are wrong regardless of what any society or individual has to say about them, we can say this. Some societies have better moral rules than others and some individuals have better personal codes than others.

If we look at the matter that way, we give up the idea of moral constraints on the social contract. If the members of a society agree that something is not wrong, then it is not wrong, regardless of whether it would be wrong according to better moral rules. And if some individuals in that society say that the rules ought to be changed, we would interpret their words the way Gilbert Harman recommends.[4] We would take them to be saying that it would be better if we changed the rules, not that we are morally obligated to change them.

But not always. Sometimes they really do mean that we are morally required to change them. In those cases, the claim is that the defective rules are inconsistent with other mutually agreed upon rules—or, more to the point, that they sanction a practice otherwise prohibited by the rules. When Martin Luther King Jr. argued against various forms of racial discrimination, he sometimes appealed to a higher authority—God—but most of his arguments appealed to atheists as well as believers. Most claimed—rightly—that the *practice* of discrimination violated shared moral *rules*. That is, he argued that discrimination is wrong not only *despite* what society said but also *because* of what society said.

The calls for change that we should interpret Harman's way are more like those of the environmental ethicists who follow Aldo Leopold.[5] They argue that the rules are defective for reasons external to our shared morality, that there is a better morality that we ought to adopt. Even if they are correct, that does not make our current behavior wrong, according to the weakened form of our third truism. That King was correct did make discrimination wrong.

What would make some moralities better than others? Kantians, of course, have an answer. The less the moral rules legitimize maxims that violate the categorical imperative, the better the rules. But Kantians would not be content to rest with the weakened version of our third truism.

So let's try another answer. Some societies, some worlds, if you will, are better than others. What makes them better? In large part, that they better enable the individuals to lead the good life. (I'll leave open for the time being whether the good life intended here is *the* good life or the good life as conceived by each individual.) In that case, a better morality is one more conducive to that kind of society.

THIS LAST PROPOSAL is just one of many proposals I've been putting forth. But it brings me to two issues I've been deliberately skirting. The first is a more inclusive account of what belongs to the social contract. Earlier, I gave what I called the bare minimum. It was more or less confined to the rules that make society possible. It should now be clear that I think there's more to it than that.

Consider this quaint old rule—"gentlemen" don't make "improper" advances to "nice girls." That society has survived without it needs no argument here. But it was part of the social contract. Nice girls expected gentlemen not to make improper advances, gentlemen knew it, and, allowing for the normal amount of backsliding, they behaved accordingly.

Not only was this rule unnecessary. It also had little, if anything, to do with resolving conflicts of interest. But what it did have a lot to do with was securing a good or decent society according to some (now outmoded) conception of good or decent.

Something else it had a lot to do with was this: Although moral rules are often worked out on a more or less ad hoc basis, they are not arbitrary. Given a shared sense of the good, plus some commonsensical assumptions about human motivation and expectation, certain kinds of agreements in certain kinds of situations naturally follow. Views about sex's role in the good life have changed, and what used to be improper advances are now often welcome. So the rules have changed. The social contract now allows men and women to make all sorts of advances. But it does not allow a man to take up too much of a woman's time—or a woman a man's—in certain situations if he—or she—is not sexually interested.

So moral rules are worked out not only to settle conflicts of interest but to advance shared conceptions of the good, not only to make society possible but to make it a good one, according to some shared conception of the good. That, of course, helps to explain changes in the rules. It also helps to explain why certain rules—allowing for variations in their application—appear to be universal among societies while others do not, both among and within societies. (The change in sexual rules has not, for example, been adopted by the so-called religious right.)

There is one other thing it helps to explain, which brings me to the other point I've been skirting. An alleged flaw of contractarian views of morality is that they can't account for certain kinds of rules—those telling us how we are to treat and not treat animals, the severely retarded, infants, or any other beings unable to enter into the social contract.

The argument goes like this: The contract can create obligations only to other members of the contract. I agree to treat you a certain way because you agree to treat me the same way. That agreement is the source of my obligations to you. The rules merely set out those obligations. Since my dog cannot agree to enter into a contract with me, there cannot be any basis for my having any obligations to it. The rules, therefore, cannot govern my treatment of it, or, for that matter, my retarded brother or infant daughter. There can be rules governing my treatment of your dog, but that is another matter. Your dog, like your car, is your property, and my obligation is to you, not it. I have agreed to treat your property in certain ways because you have agreed the same with respect to my property.

This argument may work, although I'm not sure it does, on the assumption that moral rules are restricted to those that make society possible, or that they are restricted to those intended to settle conflicts of interest among members of the contract. But they are not so restricted. They also include rules intended to make society a good society.

Most of us feel that suffering is bad. We also feel that compassion is good. So do we feel that a human life with some dignity is better than a human life with no dignity, and that a society that cares for the helpless is better than one that does not. It is only natural, then, that we would agree on rules intended to secure these goods.

The argument has another problem. Once again, moral rules are not arbitrary. Earlier, I explained that in terms of shared conceptions of the good and assumptions about human motivation and expectation. But another explanation is also available. This one involves moral coherence. For most of us, moral rules cohere because of some overarching principle, most often something like the golden rule. The rules don't follow from it, but we feel that they should at least be congruous with it. Rules that take no account of the severely retarded, say, are not.

So a contractarian view of morality can explain obligations to those unable to enter into the contract. Indeed, I think it can explain them better than other views. Kant, for example, was hard-pressed to come up with a justification for not mistreating animals, except, as Schopenhauer put it, for practice.[6] Utilitarians, on the other hand, have the opposite problem—explaining the vast differences in the rules governing our treatment of beings capable of joining the social contract and beings not so capable. These differences exist not only between rules for the treatment of humans and those for the treatment of animals but also among those for the treatment of different groups of humans. The rules do not, to give one case, allow us to treat defective ten year olds the way they allow us to treat defective newborns.

Furthermore, contractarian views best explain our attitudes about societies that, because of extreme economic hardship, have practiced infanticide. Our sympathies for the dead infants are strong, as is our regret that the hardships were so dire as to force people to kill their own children, but most of us who understand their plight do not believe they acted wrongly. On the other hand, if one group in such a society—let's call them Aryans—had decided to slaughter another—let's call them Non-Aryans—we *would* believe they acted wrongly. It is one thing to change the contract to keep the world from getting worse. It is quite another to break it so severely.

ALL THE VIEWS I'VE SKETCHED are contractarian to some extent, although the role of the social contract is different in each, more important in some than in others. Its role is most important in the externalist view, least important in the view that adopts the third truism at full strength. That view—call it the absolutist view—comes close to trivializing it. Whether it does depends on how many things are wrong despite what any society or individual has to say about them.

Truisms

Suppose that *everything* wrong is wrong regardless of what any society or individual has to say. In that case, society's rules are either the result of fitting the best morality to the needs of a particular society—some philosophers might call the process legislating for a kingdom of ends—or they are invalid.

It might seem that the internalist view, which gives ultimate moral authority to the individual rather than the social contract or something like the categorical imperative, also trivializes the social contract. It doesn't.

Remember, for most of us moral rules do provide internal reasons for acting, and we often take them to be the best reasons for acting. That in itself keeps the contract from being trivialized by internalists.

So does something else. If everything wrong is wrong regardless of what any society or individual has to say, then society's rules are otiose in moral deliberation. According to the internalist view, they are not. If they provide me with internal reasons for acting, I cannot deliberate morally unless I include them in my deliberations. Simply to ignore them whenever it suits my fancy is at least one mark of capriciousness rather than morality. (And that is at least partial payment of a promissory note issued earlier.) On the internalist view, I am morally free to ignore them only if they provide me with no internal reasons for acting.

Of course, to ignore them and to choose not to act on them in a given situation are two different things. Depending on the details, that choice may be capricious—because I deliberately discounted the weight of the rule, say—or mistaken—because further deliberation would have yielded a different result, say—or morally correct—which, on the internalist view, might be interpreted to mean keeping faith with my conception of the good.

I HOPE THAT ALL OF THE ABOVE comes off as less than earth-shattering. It was certainly meant to be less than earth-shattering. My main concerns were modest ones—to present the truisms I find so alluring, to suggest a few ways of dealing with them, and to sketch the kinds of moral theories that these ways of dealing with them can lead to. Along the way, I have issued many promissory notes and left many questions unanswered. I'll get to them after one closing thought.

The notes and questions are diverse, but all relate to a question that has always seemed to me to touch the heart of ethics. Does anybody or anything have any moral authority over how I lead *my* life? That is why this book is called *Moral Freedom*.

2

MORAL POINTS OF VIEW

MUCH OF CHAPTER 1 DEPENDS on the distinction between moral rules and what I called personal moral codes. So will much of the remaining chapters. It is, then, a distinction I take to be very important. Unfortunately, it is also one that most moral philosophers either miss or choose not to make.

Why is that? In large part, because of an identification of the moral realm with the realm of duty, or obligation, an identification that most moral philosophers attribute to Kant. Whether he deserves the full weight of responsibility for that identification is a matter I won't go into, but this much is clear. By taking duty and the moral law as his starting points, Kant left no room for a plurality of moral points of view. For him, there was only one moral point of view, and that point of view was utterly impersonal.

This identification has been accepted not only by philosophers of a Kantian bent—those who, among other things, constantly talk of *the* moral point of view—but even by his critics. Nietzsche, for example—at least on one reading of him—considered himself an immoralist because he believed in the supremacy of personal values over impersonal rules. And R. M. Hare, who considers the source of all values to be personal, still distinguishes moral from other values on Kantian grounds. Moral values, he holds, must issue judgments that are both universalizable and overriding. And Gilbert Harman, who is both an internalist and a relativist, also puts a Kantian requirement on morality.[1] Although he does not require that moral judgments be universalizable or overriding, he does claim that to act morally is to act out of Kantian respect.

This way of looking at morality has some very specific consequences. Questions of the good life are either read out of ethics or given a back seat to questions of moral obligation. What I ought to do supersedes how I shall live my life. At the extreme, pursuit of personal ideals is relegated to the area of self-interest: one is either egoistic or moral, acts according to reasons of self-interest or moral imperatives, is an immoralist or takes *the* moral point of view.

Chapter 1, on the other hand, assumed that there are two moral points of view, the personal and impersonal. That is why I used the awkward phrase "reasons provided by moral rules" instead of the standard "moral reasons." Now is the time to justify that assumption.

I LIKE TO WRITE AND I LIKE TO READ, to have a gin or two before dinner while I listen to Mozart, to take weekends in cities that have a variety of good restaurants, plus pleasant hotels and good museums and orchestras. I also like to be a *mensch* with family and friends. I also like television reruns of old sitcoms that appear after the late night news.

None of that is remarkable. Nor is it remarkable that some of these things are more important to me than others. Nor is it remarkable that some of the things that are more important than others provide less pleasure than the same others. Nor is it re-markable that I occasionally backslide, that I have to remind myself that importance has been overwhelmed by pleasure, or that I have been living more of a convenient life than a valuable one.

Put another way, I have a variety of dispositions. Some are means to value—that is, are ways of getting pleasure—and others are sources of value—that is, give me values that are specific to those dispositions, values I would not have if I did not have those dis-positions. The second kind is the more important. Neglecting to have a gin or watch "Barney Miller" is not backsliding. It is merely to forego a pleasure. Neglecting a manuscript is. That is why I might take a manuscript to Chicago with me and spend a few hours working on it in my hotel room while my wife is out doing things I would rather be doing with her, but not stay in my room to watch "Barney Miller."

I do not feel any *obligation* to work on the manuscript in such cases (unless I am stretching a contract deadline beyond accepta-bility), and I am not following a self-imposed *rule*. Certainly, I would not tell my wife to go on without me because my *duty* requires that I stay in the room. And just as certainly, neither universalizability nor respect for persons plays any role in my deliberations. But it would be most misleading to characterize my motives as egoistic, or to say that I was acting out of self-interest, or to say that my deliberations and behavior were morally neutral. I stay in my room so as not to backslide. I stay in my room because I believe that if I don't, I will fail to live up to certain values I hold. If I leave, I compromise my conception of the good.

Of course, I rarely take a manuscript to Chicago with me. The values in question do not require specific actions or kinds of actions at specific times. Rather, they provide a general framework against which I measure my life as a whole. The dispositions that are the source of these values are the dispositions that I try to strengthen. They are the ones that make my life meaningful, the ones that make my life mine. They are my most important projects, what Williams calls my *ground* projects.[2]

WHAT I'VE BEEN TALKING ABOUT is my personal moral code—the values that constitute my conception of the good life. It is personal because it's *my* conception, based on *my* projects and commitments. And it is moral because it is based on *reflection* on my projects and commitments, and because it concerns the *good* life, not mere prudence or self-interest or whim or unreflective pursuit of pleasure, and because it admits of *backsliding*, and because it provides the measure against which I judge the *worth* of my life, and because it encompasses deeply held *principles*, not mere preferences.

I'm not sure that "code" is the best word for it. I use it only because I cannot think of a better one. But I am sure that what I've been talking about is not a set of rules. Personal moral codes do not, again, require particular actions or kinds of actions at particular times. They neither define nor regulate practices. Nor are they the sort of thing individuals obey. Rather, they are ideals, the sort of thing we can be more or less faithful to.

Moral rules, on the other hand, are impersonal. They are intended to define and regulate practices for the common good, independent of any individual's personal projects. Moral rules are intended to give everyone reasons to act. My personal code gives me alone reasons to act.

THE SORT OF REASONING I've been talking about is not, I said, egoistic or self-interested, even though it is about *my* projects. To say that is to recognize a distinction between self-interest and self-worth. It is to recognize that the desire to lead a worthy life is different from the desire to satisfy one's interests. It is to recognize that trying to live according to one's conception of the good life is not a matter of maximizing personal utility.

It is also to recognize that one's projects are as likely to be altruistic as not. Being a *mensch* is, after all, a part of many people's conception of the good life, which is why they concern themselves less with their obligations toward friends and family than with what would be nice to do for them. (A *mensch* does not, for example, help a friend out of a jam because it is his duty, nor would he ask himself, if the circumstances arose, whether it is right to lie in order to save a loved one's life. Kant, who thought that being a *mensch* had nothing to do with morality, was apparently not one.) Moreover, one's projects can extend beyond friends and family, which is why we occasionally see photographs of former president Jimmy Carter wielding a hammer in various impoverished communities.

I also said that the sort of reasoning I've been talking about is not morally neutral. On standard accounts, it is. From the moral point of view, standard accounts have it, my decision to stay in the hotel room falls into the category of the permissible. I have neither an obligation to stay there nor one to accompany my wife. On my account, it is morally neutral only from one moral point of view, the impersonal one. From the other, the personal one, it is a matter of great moral significance.

BEFORE I BEGAN STUDYING PHILOSOPHY, the truth of that last sentence was obvious to me. Two years ago I would have argued against it. Indeed, I did argue against it—in my ethics class. The argument was based on an analogy to etiquette, and it went like this:

Every morning Jones has a few cups of coffee after his shower.

He is still in his bathrobe, and he does not care whether it is open. Nor does he care whether he slurps his coffee, blows his nose at the table, scratches himself wherever he pleases, curses out loud if something he reads angers him or emits a long, satisfying burp. Suppose he decides that he does care. Suppose he gets it into his head that this is the way one ought to have one's coffee in the morning, and decides that from then on he will always leave his robe open while having his morning coffee, and that he will blow his nose, scratch, curse, slurp and burp. Does he now have a personal etiquette?

The answer, of course, was no. Jones is not following any rules. He's simply doing what he wants to do. Imagine him, if you will, joining colleagues at a local restaurant one morning and justifying his open robe and the rest as being a matter of personal etiquette. Etiquette is a matter of agreed upon rules, not of doing what one wants to do.

So, the argument went, is it with morality. There can no more be a personal moral code than there can be a personal etiquette.

The argument depends, of course, on an identification of morality with moral rules, and that is something I no longer accept. But it also depends on something else—the idea that all wants are of a piece. They aren't.

To be sure, wants have at least this much in common. We want something because we like it (or think we will like it) or because it will get us something we like (or we think that it will). And it may even be the case that to discover that we like something is to discover that it gives us pleasure. But, upon reflection, we can also discover something else. Some of our likes are just pleasant ways to pass time (watching "Barney Miller," for example), others just pleasant ways to satisfy basic needs (eating northern Italian food, for example), others just pleasant breaks from routine (taking a weekend in Chicago, for example), while others have become for us sources of value other than pleasure, give our lives worth, and take on a guiding role that the others do not.

These last desires are what Williams calls categorical desires, the ones capable of providing an answer to the question, Why go on?[3] They are, he perceptively notes, the ones that are not contingent on our being alive, because they are capable of settling the issue whether to remain alive. They are also the foundations of our ground projects, which we may in turn characterize as the projects whose value is not contingent on our being alive. A world in which I do not eat striped bass is a world worse than one in which I do, only if I am in that world. (If that sounds either paradoxical or incoherent, try it another way. A world without a me who eats striped bass is no worse than a world without a me who does not eat striped bass, but a world with a me who eats striped bass is better than a world with a me who doesn't.)

One cannot imagine that the older Matisse, who turned to making paper cutouts when he could no longer paint, felt the same way about a world without Matisse making art. Nor could one imagine that immigrant tailors who sent their children to American universities felt the same way about a world in which they did not make their Atlantic crossings. If they, and Matisse, were merely doing what they wanted, then merely doing what one wants when one eats striped bass cannot mean the same thing.

WITH THESE POINTS IN MIND, let's now turn to what I've been calling the externalist view of morality. According to that view, individuals can have reasons to act even if those reasons are incapable of motivating them. These reasons are impersonal reasons, the kind of reasons that apply to everyone, regardless of their desires, commitments, and projects. Moreover, it is possible to rank all reasons for acting independent of any individual's desires, commitments, and projects. Some reasons are better than others, and any individual who does not recognize which ones those are is mistaken, exhibiting a failure of practical reason, and any such individual who cannot be convinced otherwise is being irrational.

Among the reasons that apply to everyone are the reasons provided by moral rules—or, I should say, so as not to beg any questions, reasons provided by valid moral rules. These reasons are also the best reasons.

Externalists tend to argue in two ways. The first is to identify the moral point of view with the impersonal view, to say that to reason morally is to consider how anyone in the same situation ought to act, which amounts to asking what the valid moral rules require. But that, I have been arguing, is only a part of moral reasoning, one kind of moral reasoning. To make it all of moral reasoning, the only kind, is to beg the whole issue of moral freedom and authority.

It is important to see precisely how it begs that issue. In particular, it is important to see that the way it begs the issue has nothing to do with externalism per se or the claim that the reasons provided by moral rules are the best reasons.

Consider the question raised by Baier: Why should we be moral? That question he takes to be equivalent to this one: Why should we take the moral point of view? And that one he takes to be equivalent to this one: Why should we act on the reasons provided by moral rules?

Baier has an answer to his question—moral rules provide the best reasons. But suppose he didn't have an answer. In that case, he would not be an externalist, because he would have to concede that some people do not have reason to follow moral rules. But the fact remains that they would not be moral. That is, they might have the *intellectual* freedom to reject moral rules (they are not irrational in doing so) but they do not have the *moral* freedom to reject moral rules (they are immoral, or, perhaps, amoral in doing so).

Now it may be that the moral life requires that one follow moral rules, but if it does, an argument showing that it does is in order.

IS THERE SUCH AN ARGUMENT? Oddly enough, one place to look is Williams's *Ethics and the Limits of Philosophy*—oddly, because Williams is no supporter of the hegemony of moral rules.[4] But the book does distinguish the ethical from the moral, with the ethical including but not being restricted to the moral. He justifies the distinction in part by the words' respective Greek and Latin roots, and in part by Western philosophical usage. What is distinctively moral by this distinction is the area of obligation, duty, the *ought*. And that area, in terms of the discussion of this chapter, is the area of moral rules.

I have no quarrel with that distinction as a technical one. If I made the same distinction, I would recast my arguments much as Williams casts his, in terms of different ethical—as opposed to moral—perspectives. But philosophers' distinctions are not always the distinctions of the common person, and in this case, the common person is more likely to distinguish the moral from the ethical in a very different way. According to that distinction, ethics is a fairly legalistic area, one that typically includes official ethical codes and adjudicative bodies that determine whether individuals subject to the codes have committed any infractions of them. Thus, we have legal *ethics* as opposed to legal *morality* and speak of *unethical* lawyers as opposed to *immoral* ones. On the other hand, we are more likely to hear of sexual *morality* than sexual *ethics*, even when

Moral Points of View

the issue is not one of sexual duty but sexual values. Then again, many people—including many philosophers—assume that, in the widest context, they talk of the same thing when they talk of ethics and when they talk of morality. I have always belonged to this last group.

Not that I think there's anything to settle here. (*Webster's New Collegiate Dictionary*, for example, accommodates all three of the above views.) What I do think, though, is this: Williams's distinction, however convenient for certain philosophical purposes, does not answer any important questions, but merely provides a way of posing them, a point that Williams is well aware of. Certainly, it cannot answer ours: Is there one proper relationship between impersonal reasons and certain kinds of personal reasons in the moral (or ethical) life of the individual?

ANOTHER PLACE TO LOOK for the required argument is our first truism, which must be slightly recast if it is to help. Suppose we say that *morality* is a social institution rather than that moral *rules* are society's rules. This can be taken as an empirical discovery, as the historically minded Nietzsche and a host of anthropologists have taken it, or a conceptual point, as Baier seems to take it.[5] Either way, the result is the same. If all of morality is a social institution, then the proper role of moral rules in the moral life of the individual is to be worked out socially. It is not a purely personal matter, as it may be if only part of morality—moral rules—is a social institution. It is a matter to be decided from the impersonal point of view.

This line is more promising than the first. There may even be something to it. But it does have problems. The most important is this. Both Nietzsche and Baier reach their shared conclusion because of their focus on moral rules. That is, they go from the discovery (or recognition) that moral rules are society's rules to the more general claim that morality is a social institution. If they had begun with a conception of morality that included personal moral codes, that step would have been much more difficult.

It is worth asking what would legitimize such a step. The answer, I think, is an argument that an individual's conception of the good life counts as a *moral* conception of the good life only if it incorporates some societally shared conception of the good. That is, moral goods cannot be based solely on individual projects, but require a social basis as well.

I also think that the possibility of such an argument can be found in the notion of an individual's ground project, which I have characterized as a project whose value is not contingent on that individual's being alive and is thus the source of the worth and meaning of that individual's life.

Such a characterization does suggest that the value of my ground projects does not rest solely on my own dispositions. Certainly, they would not be *my* projects unless I were appropriately disposed. But would they be my *ground* projects if they had no value for anyone else? Recall the older Matisse and the immigrant tailor. Perhaps it is no accident that their ground projects involved widely shared values. Nor, perhaps, is it an accident that these values, while not given supreme importance by everybody—or in Matisse's case, by many—are still considered to be of some importance by many. If I am to reflect on my various projects, if I am to discover that some are valuable for reasons other than the pleasure they give, that they are a source of value, worth, and meaning, then, however personal my reasoning may be, it seems that I must also be regarding myself as a member of a community with shared values. If a project is to be the ground of my life's worth, then I must see its value as lying both within and without me. To put the matter in the form of what I hope is a self-answering question, can someone's ground project be nose-picking?

Although this line of reasoning can get us pretty far, whether it can get us far enough is doubtful. For one thing, the community with which one identifies need not be—nor, in many cases, is it likely to be—all of society. For another, it may not even be part of the wider moral community. One may, for example, identify oneself with a group of outlaws. Moreover, one may not even identify with an existing community. Think of Don Quixote, who identified with a community that no longer existed, or Nietzsche's Zarathustra, who identified with one that did not yet exist. This last example is particularly important. It shows that, despite what may be true in the previous paragraph, one can have as one's ground project the "transvaluation of values."

Given these considerations, what is left of the claim that morality (not just moral rules) is a social institution? In the matter of personal moral codes, only this—that they presuppose a conception of shared values. But as long as those values need not be society's values, we cannot conclude that an individual's conception of the good life counts as a *moral* conception of the good life only if it incorporates some societally shared conception of the good. And if we cannot conclude that, we cannot conclude that the moral life requires us to abide by society's rules.

We can, however, reach a weaker conclusion—that the moral life requires that we *consider* moral rules. That is a conclusion we'd be entitled to even without the foregoing considerations. After all, the moral life includes two perspectives, the personal and the impersonal. Although we cannot say that an individual whose moral life does not include the impersonal has no morality, we can certainly say that he has a diminished morality. The issue at hand is not, I should stress, whether the impersonal view can be read out of the moral life. It can't—any more than the personal view can be. Rather, the issue is whether individuals have the moral freedom to decide for themselves how to balance the demands of moral obligations against their own conceptions of the good life.

Although the conclusion that the moral life requires consideration of moral rules can be reached without the considerations of the previous section, those considerations do give it some personal bite. I have my conception of the good life not only because of my own projects, but also because I identify with a community whose values I share. My values are not just personal, then, but interpersonal as well. The interpersonal is not, to be sure, the same as the impersonal. The former is the realm of *us* (however many that may be), the latter of *anyone*. But identifying with some community is likely to provide an individual with some disposition to treat its members in certain ways, and that is likely to include taking some obligations to them into account.

IF THE MORAL LIFE DOES NOT REQUIRE us to follow moral rules, does something else? The externalists' answer is yes—practical reason does. The reasons provided by moral rules are the best reasons for acting.

Various arguments have been marshaled in support of this conclusion. For the present, I shall deal with the most widely discussed argument, one that Baier has offered in various forms.[6] The argument, which is based on Hobbes's state of nature argument, begins with a situation in which the result of everyone's pursuing his own interest is that no one's interest is served. Such a situation is the prisoner's dilemma.

Butch and Sundance are arrested for train robbery. They are held in separate cells. Here's what the sheriff tells Butch. If Butch confesses and Sundance doesn't, Butch will not serve time—he'll be rewarded for implicating Sundance—but Sundance will get twenty years. If, on the other hand, Sundance does confess, they will both get ten. If Butch does not confess and Sundance doesn't either, then they can't be convicted of train robbery, but both will get two years on a lesser charge. But if Sundance does confess, then Sundance gets off and Butch gets twenty years. The sheriff has already told Sundance the same thing, and he tells Butch so.

Butch reasons like this: Either Sundance confesses or he doesn't. Either way, Butch comes off better if he himself does—ten years versus twenty if Sundance does confess, freedom versus two years if Sundance doesn't. So he confesses. So does Sundance, who has reasoned the same way. And they each get ten years—eight more than they would have got if neither had confessed. Clearly, it would have been better for both Butch and Sundance if they'd been able to work out a deal between them that neither would confess.

That kind of deal is analogous to our moral rules. Without moral rules, we would all act for reasons of self-interest, as Butch and Sundance do. The result, as it was for Butch and Sundance, would be in nobody's interest. Therefore, it is in everyone's interest to work out a system of rules that we can count on others to adhere to. That's what makes the reasons provided by these rules the best reasons. It is in the interest of everyone that we act on them.

It takes little insight to realize that once the rules have been adopted, matters have changed. If Butch can count on Sundance to live up to the bargain, then it is in his interest to confess. He gets off. (Poor Sundance, unfortunately, gets twenty years.) Why, then, isn't that a better reason to act than the reason provided by their bargain? More generally, why aren't my own reasons of self-interest better than reasons provided by moral rules when I know that others will follow the rules?

The answer, of course, is that if everyone felt that way, we'd all be back in the situation of the prisoner's dilemma. And the response, of course, is that everyone does *not* feel that way. What this response shows is that what counts as the best reason depends on what perspective somebody takes—the impersonal perspective or the perspective of self-interest. From the first, impersonal reasons are the best. From the second, reasons of self-interest are the best. That is not a surprising result. Nor is it surprising that it undermines the entire argument. To argue for the impersonal perspective from the impersonal perspective is to beg the issue, which I am hardly the first to point out.

On the other hand, to say that the answer is undermined is not to say that it is dead. What is needed to save it is a theory of practical reason showing that the impersonal point of view is better than the personal. Baier has one. It is an externalist theory of practical reason, one that claims that people can have external reasons for acting. Whether they can is the issue I'll consider in the next chapter.

BEFORE TURNING TO THE NEXT CHAPTER, though, I want to point out another feature of the prisoner's dilemma, one that has not, as far as I know, been discussed anywhere else.

Suppose that Butch and Sundance have agreed that neither will confess if they're caught. Suppose further that they are caught, and while Butch bides his time in his cell he comes across and reads a copy of *Crime and Punishment*. (An unlikely story, I know, but please bear with me.) He is greatly impressed by the book, especially by the final pages, which set up the promise of Raskolnikov's ultimate regeneration. He begins to reflect upon his life and it begins to dawn on him that he, too, is in need of regeneration.

He has not, he now sees, led a worthwhile life. What bothers him is not that he has spent most of it in violation of society's rules. Robbing trains gave him much pleasure. So did spending what he stole. What bothers him instead is that the robbing and the spending gave him nothing else—no family, no home, no stake in the future. Should the sheriff walk into the cell and put a bullet in his head, it would make no difference to him. What does it matter if he never robs another train or never visits another bordello?

Soon he finds himself envying the people he robbed, the people who were building the communities he merely passed through, people whose lives had a worth that his did not. He discovers that he wants to live among them, to be one of them, even to begin following the rules that they follow. But he does not feel worthy to live among them. What will make him feel worthy? Confessing.

So he confesses. Sundance gets twenty years and Butch walks. Soon he opens a general store, marries the mayor's daughter, and fathers two children, one who will eventually go off to Harvard and one to Radcliffe.

DID BUTCH DO WRONG? Well, he did break his agreement with Sundance. Indeed, as I told the story, he didn't even consider it. Nor did he consider all the options available to him—like confessing without implicating Sundance, in which case he might have got ten years but Sundance only two. I could add such things, but then I'd have to add a lot more—a desire on Butch's part to protect his new community from Sundance, for example—and by then I'd have a Chekhov-sized novella. Even with that, I'm not sure we'd have a ready answer to the question.

So let's change the question. If what Butch did was wrong, was he being immoral? For many people, that question is probably as difficult as the first—in large part, because there is at least good reason for answering no. Butch's reason for confessing was to make himself worthy of living among the people whose values he'd come to share. It was not to avoid prison. In fact, he would have chosen to confess regardless of his confession's effect on his time in prison.

And that brings me to the feature of the prisoner's dilemma I want to point out—how far removed it is from the full reality of our moral lives. It gives us two people who have only one concern—spending as little time in prison as they can—and then concludes that they would both be better off if they agreed to cooperate. We don't even know whether they're guilty. (Of course, by calling them Butch and Sundance, I led you to believe they were. But I also led you to believe they had all the good-natured charm of Newman and Redford.)

This removal from reality can be justified on the assumption that there are two kinds of reasons, moral reasons and reasons of self-interest, where moral reasons are the reasons provided by moral rules and reasons of self-interest include all the rest. Assuming that, we can then say (from the impersonal point of view, at least) that moral reasons are the best reasons. We can then work back to the reality of our moral lives by adding complications—most notably, conflicts among moral rules in particular circumstances. (The idea, apparently, bears similarity to that of physics. Begin with frictionless surfaces and no outside forces to get the basic principle of motion—inertia—and then complicate matters by adding other forces that get us back to the real world.)

But the complications I added to Butch's dilemma had nothing to do with conflicting moral rules. I did not even have him think that he had a moral obligation to protect the community from thieves. Instead, I had him think that he wanted to, because it was now his community. What Butch was really thinking about, then, was not the right but the good. And the question he was trying to answer was not an impersonal one—what ought one do?—but a very personal one. He was trying to decide how to live his life.

Of course, the prisoner's dilemma can be recast to accommodate such considerations, and in its recast form it would show that impersonal reasons provided by moral rules are better than personal reasons provided by our conceptions of the good life. One can hardly imagine oneself living the good life in the state of nature.

But for many people, the recast argument would be far less compelling. They are the people who put moral rules ahead of self-interest because to do so is part of their conceptions of the good life—people who believe, for example, that a rich life is better than a middle-income life, but not if they have to resort to armed robbery to get it. They are, in short, the people who believe they have good reason to follow moral rules, regardless of the prisoner's dilemma. Such people would find it difficult to believe that they had good reason to follow them if doing so meant a sacrifice of self-worth.

In the next chapter, we'll see if they're right.

3

REASONS

CHAPTER 2 BEGAN WITH THE OBSERVATION that much of the first chapter—much of the book, for that matter—hinges on there being two moral points of view. If the impersonal point of view were the only one, the issue of the moral hegemony of moral rules as I have posed it could not arise. The area of individual moral freedom would automatically be narrowed to the range allowed by the weakened version of the second truism. It would consist of decisions left undecided by the rules.

The issue of the *intellectual* hegemony of moral rules, however, would remain. We could still ask whether reason requires us to follow them. The answer would not be of distinctively moral importance—it would not affect our moral appraisals of individuals and their actions, for example—but it would still be of philosophical importance.

But the impersonal point of view is not the only moral point of view. And that means that the issue of the intellectual hegemony of moral rules is of great moral importance. If reason requires us to follow moral rules, then, just as surely as if there were no personal moral point of view, our moral freedom would be restricted to the range allowed by the weakened version of the second truism. So our answer to the question *will* affect our moral appraisals of agents.

Reasons

THIS LAST POINT IS LIKELY to be missed by philosophers who talk of *the* moral point of view. So is another point, which is likely to be missed by most philosophers who are accustomed to discussing the claim that reasons provided by moral rules are the best reasons for acting. What an extraordinary claim that is!

It is, I'm convinced, just as extraordinary as Berkeley's claim that tables and chairs are not made of matter. And it is, I'm equally convinced, extraordinary for the same reason: it runs totally afoul of the conventional wisdom of ordinary men and women. When people break a promise or tell a lie merely for their own convenience—and does anybody know anybody who hasn't?—even those who freely admit that they did wrong will maintain that they did so for good reason.

Of course, they may be mistaken, just as freshman logic students mistakenly go from denying the antecedent to denying the consequent. But notice—how many of us have found our students to be stubborn on that point? I have yet to meet one who hasn't been convinced by one telling example. (If I go out into the rain I'll get wet. I don't go out into the rain. But what if I take a shower instead?) On the other hand, they can be—and often are—very stubborn about the reasonableness of the prisoner who breaks his agreement not to confess. His morality they are quite willing to question, but as for his reasonableness—that they take to be ironclad.

That does not, I realize, make them right. After all, they're equally stubborn about arguments against free will. But my point is not that they're right. It is merely that the claim in question is an extraordinary one. (Then again, so is the claim that there's no free will.)

Here's something else that makes it extraordinary. When epistemologists, philosophers of mind, and philosophers of science debate epistemic rationality, they take conventional notions of rationality as their starting point. Although extreme skeptics (another group that makes an extraordinary claim) may end up denying that we have any rational justification for believing anything, the usual practice is to show what makes ordinary rationality rational. The various answers (foundationalism and coherentism being the most common) do not seek to turn ordinary rationality on its head. Rather, they seek to explain it. And although one group may think the other unreasonable for not accepting arguments that it takes to be conclusive, it does not think that the nonbelievers are doomed to unreasonableness in the rest of their lives.

Philosophers who claim that reasons provided by moral rules are the best reasons, on the other hand, are claiming—however implicitly—that their opponents *are* doomed to unreasonableness in the rest of their lives. If I put some other reason ahead of a moral reason, I am being unreasonable. Of course, they are too polite to say that. (Baier, for example, prefers to say that I am acting contrary to reason.) But however put, the claim goes a lot farther and a lot deeper than the foundationalist's claim that I don't understand why my belief that there is a typewriter before me can be justified only if I have some other beliefs that are self-justifying.

For precisely the same reasons, the claim that individuals can have external reasons for acting is an extraordinary (although not thereby false) claim. Tell an ordinary fifty-five-year-old mortal who likes his beer, popcorn, and television and has no interest in broadening his mind that he ought to go to the opera because it will do just that and see what kind of response you get. If he is willing to say anything more than "So what?" it is likely to be something to the effect that just because *you* have a reason to go to the opera doesn't mean that *he* does. Then try telling him that your own tastes have nothing to do with it. It's not just that he or you ought to go to the opera, but that "one" ought to go to the opera because it will broaden "one's" mind. *Then* see what kind of response you get.

THE PURPOSE OF THE LAST COUPLE OF PAGES was to drive home a simple but often neglected point. Ambitious theories of practical reason can take us very far from conventional wisdom. Less ambitious theories, on the other hand, are more like their epistemological counterparts. They keep us fairly close to conventional wisdom. Harman, for example, thinks of practical reasoning as being much like epistemic reasoning. The only difference is that intentions and desires are added to the process. On his account, to engage in practical reasoning is to make minimal modification of one's antecedent beliefs and intentions in the interest of explanatory coherence and the satisfaction of intrinsic desires.[1]

What makes his account so unambitious is that it is primarily an *explanatory* account. That is, it is an account of what we do when we decide to do something. And that is precisely what the more ambitious theories object to. Practical reasoning, they say, has a normative as well as an explanatory side, and an account like Harman's misses the normative.

But does it? His account does give the function of practical reasoning—attainment of explanatory coherence and satisfaction of intrinsic desires—and that certainly seems to suggest a way of distinguishing good from bad practical reasoning. But, the objection goes, primarily explanatory accounts are accounts only of *relative* rationality. They tell us what is rational relative to an agent's beliefs and desires, but not what it is to be rational, period.

But why should we think there's any more to rationality than what such accounts tell us? Why should we think that there must be some absolute norm when it comes to practical reasoning? Or, for that matter, why should we think that the norm of achieving explanatory coherence and satisfaction of intrinsic desires is not absolute enough?

It will do no good here to attempt a comparison with epistemic rationality, because Harman's theory of practical reasoning is nothing but his theory of epistemic reasoning with intentions and desires added. What is epistemically rational is what maximizes explanatory coherence with minimal modification of antecedent beliefs. That is, when we reason epistemically, we ought to maximize explanatory coherence in a way that allows us best to conserve antecedent beliefs. The physicist who reasons as she ought to reason does self-consciously what the brain does automatically when it processes information that light carries to the retina. When we deliberate practically, we do self-consciously what the brain does automatically when the processed information is that a car is coming toward us.

And that is why reasoning (both epistemic and practical) has its explanatory and normative sides. When we deliberate self-consciously, we have to ask ourselves what the desired results are and how best to achieve them. We have to ask ourselves if we've covered the relevant bases, if neglected considerations would be of use, if modification of our desires is in order. What explains in some cases guides in others.

And in still other cases it justifies. How do I justify my beliefs? By giving the reasoning that led to them or could have led to them. How do I justify my actions? By giving the reasoning that led to them or could have led to them. The "could have" in each sentence is there for two reasons. First, our explanations of our own beliefs and actions involve a good deal of theorizing about ourselves. We may—and no doubt often are—wrong. Second, if you don't look at things the same way I do—that is, if we don't share all the relevant beliefs and desires— I am likely to try to produce some reasoning that you will find acceptable. That is why philosophers offer other philosophers many more reasons for a favored position than they needed to convince themselves of its rightness.

OUR OBJECTORS ARE NOT LIKELY to be satisfied with any of this. The thought persists that internalist accounts like Harman's put practical and epistemic reasoning on different footings, that they relativize the practical in a way that the epistemic cannot be relativized. If something is a reason for me to act, internalist accounts have it, then it is not necessarily a reason for anyone else to act, but if something is a reason for me to believe something, objectors say, then surely it must be a reason for anybody to believe the same thing.

But that is mistaken. Whether something is a reason for me to believe something depends on my antecedent beliefs. If you have different antecedent beliefs, then it is perfectly possible that what will be rational for me to accept will not be rational for you to accept. Since our relevant antecedent beliefs are usually alike, that does not often arise in the usual course of events. But it is by no means rare in very theoretically charged clashes—Einstein versus Bohr, for instance, or Chomsky versus Skinner, or Berkeley versus Locke, or Nietzsche versus Kant.

But won't one side of the dispute be mistaken? Perhaps, but what is true does not always coincide with what is rational for somebody to believe. (Suppose, as physicists generally believe, Bohr was right. Does anybody *really* want to say that Bohr was being more *reasonable* than Einstein?) Then again, it may be that the notion of truth plays no extra-theoretical role in such disputes. Einstein, for example, believed that there was no one best physical theory and that truth could be specified only from within some theory that met certain tests of acceptability (which quantum physics, he believed, did not). Many contemporary philosophers of science agree. And many feel the same way about commonsense "theories" about middle-sized objects like tables and chairs.

Whether those (admittedly extraordinary) claims are to be accepted is not for me to decide here. But here's a related (nonextraordinary) claim. It is extremely difficult to find a philosopher of science or epistemologist who will say that there is such a thing as an epistemically best kind of reason that can be specified extra-theoretically. Evidentiary reasons are the best reasons, of course, but that in itself is vacuous. What counts as an evidentiary reason must be decided from within a theory. Moreover, it is probably impossible to find one who will say that I have reason q to believe that p when 'p because q' coheres with none of my beliefs. Aristotle had no reason to believe that certain syllogisms that are valid by his canons are invalid. Those of us who take modern predicate logic as a matter of course have very good reason to believe it. So *would* have Aristotle, if he had shared the relevant beliefs. But he didn't.

If internalism is to be refuted, then, it cannot be on any analogy to epistemic reasoning.

LET'S LOOK AT ANOTHER APPROACH, then, one taken by Baier.[2] This one argues that practical reasoning does not conclude with an intention (or decision or action) but with a judgment that the agent ought to do such and such. Whether the agent acquires the intention to do such and such, on this view, is not a task of practical reason. The task of practical reason is merely to determine what the agent ought to do—what Baier calls the cognitive task. The task of acquiring the relevant intention is to mold the will to the conclusion— what Baier calls the executive task.

The importance of this move is readily apparent. By separating the cognitive and executive tasks, Baier separates reasons from motivations altogether. Reasons belong to the cognitive task, while motivations belong to the executive. So whether a reason is capable of motivating me has nothing to do with whether it is *my* reason. Any reason that is relevant to the task of deciding what I ought to do is one of my reasons regardless of whether it is capable of motivating me. And whatever kind of reason proves to be decisive in answering the question is the best kind of reason.

Equally important is this point. Once practical reason is removed from my own motivations, it becomes utterly impersonal. What I ought to do is what any similarly placed individual ought to do. What is a reason for any similarly placed individual to act is a reason for me to act. And the best reasons to act are the best reasons for any similarly placed individual to act.

There is something intuitively implausible about this bifurcation. For one thing, in most of my practical deliberations I do not ask myself what *anyone* ought to do, but what is best for *me* to do. For example, I just got up and poured myself another cup of coffee. I began with an intention—to drink coffee—and acquired a new belief—my cup is empty—and arrived at a new intention—to get up, walk to the pot, and pour. It is hard to isolate any cognitive and executive tasks in the process. The whole thing seems much as Harman describes it.

But that implausibility does not seriously hurt Baier's case. When we look at practical reasoning as an explanation of someone's behavior, Harman's analysis does not meet with serious objection from Baier. It is the normative role of practical reasoning that requires the bifurcation. Unfortunately, even in that role Baier's view is implausible.

Often I do ask what I ought to do from the impersonal point of view. That, of course, is when I have some concern to do what is morally right. But I don't always stop when I have found an answer. Sometimes I'll deliberate about whether I should do what the answer says I should do. (Following moral rules is not my *only* concern.) Notice the word "deliberate" here. Baier may call that the executive task if he so chooses, but as long as I'm still deliberating about what to do, it certainly *seems* that I'm engaging in practical reasoning.

But Baier has an answer here, too. Practical reasoning cannot end with an intention, for two reasons. First, reasoning must end with something that can be formulated in a *that*-clause, and intentions cannot be formulated that way. Second, the conclusion of practical reasoning must be reachable by anyone, not just the agent deliberating about his own actions. But only I can intend my own actions.

I don't think either of those claims is correct, but it really doesn't matter. Even if both are true, they won't do the trick. All we need do is change the conclusion from an intention to "The best thing for Olen to do is pour himself a cup of coffee" or ". . . keep his promise to his wife" or whatever. (Please, do *not* read "The best thing for Olen to do" as "What best promotes Olen's self-interest." The best thing for an individual to do may be—and for many individuals often is—what one ought to do.) Assuming that I am disposed to do what I take to be the best thing for me to do—why else would I stop when I get there?—my intention immediately follows. Certainly, it is more plausible to suppose that the intention immediately follows the conclusion than to suppose that there is some intermediate reasoning that is not to be counted as *practical* reasoning. (What other kind of reasoning could it be?)

Of course, someone else reasoning about what's best for me to do may reach a different conclusion. And if there is one and only one thing that is the best thing for me to do, one of us may be mistaken. And if the mistake is mine, and if it is due to the fact that I discounted some particular class of reasons, haven't I acted contrary to reason? Maybe, but the conclusion concerns what's best for *me* to do, not what *one* ought to do. When phrased that way, it's difficult to say that my own projects—including my ground projects—must play a secondary role if I am to act according to reason.

We can say that only if practical reason ends with a conclusion about what *one* ought to do. Even more important, we can say that I can have external reasons for acting only if practical reason stops there—only, that is, if we separate reason from motivation. But if it ends in either an intention or a judgment that is causally and directly linked to an intention, then what can be the grounds for making such an extraordinary claim? Only this—the assumption that the best thing for me or anybody else to do is always what one ought to do. But that is as much a moral assumption as it is an assumption about reasoning. (Let it be to John Rawls's everlasting credit that he takes the "original position" to be a matter of fairness, not rationality.) It is also an assumption that I often make in my practical deliberations. But it doesn't prove anything.

I TURNED TO BAIER'S VIEWS on practical reason to see if they could save his prisoner's dilemma argument. It is easy to see the connection between those views and his argument's conclusion. Why is the best reason from the impersonal point of view *the* best reason? Because practical reasoning must be done from the impersonal point of view.

If what I've been saying is correct, though, it doesn't. A full moral life may require that we take the impersonal view into account in our practical deliberations, but reason does not require that everybody—regardless of motivations—do so, let alone that everybody—regardless of motivations—act on its dictates.

However, it is no doubt true that reason requires most of us to take it into account. Most of us do, once again, desire to do the morally right thing. So if we are to determine what the best thing for us to do is on some occasion, we are more likely to arrive at a correct answer if we include reasons that Baier says everyone ought to act on.

On the other hand, we seem to have reached the conclusion that someone who has no such intrinsic desire has no reason to include them in his deliberations. But we haven't. Even the egoist might find it in his interest to do the morally right thing—in order to impress a woman he wants to seduce, for example—so he will have to ask himself what one ought to do if he is to achieve his purpose.

But we might have to grant even more than that. To deny that an individual can have external reasons for acting is one thing. To determine whether something is a reason for an individual to act (and from now on an individual's reason for acting is the same thing as an individual's internal reason for acting, since there is no other kind) is another.

HERE'S THE PROBLEM. Something is a reason for an individual to act only if it is capable of motivating him. But what, exactly, does that mean? Capability is a modal notion, and, like other modal notions, it is very hard to pin down. Under the appropriate circumstances, *anything* can motivate me to do almost anything. So if internalism is to have any teeth, some restriction must be put on the appropriate circumstances.

Bernard Williams, whose arguments I have been supporting (but not reproducing) in this chapter, attempts to do just that.[3] He begins

49

with what he calls an individual's subjective motivation set. Although he doesn't give a precise account of a motivation set, the general idea is that it contains a variety of dispositions—desires, intentions, patterns of emotional reaction, personal loyalties, projects and commitments, and at least some kinds of beliefs, most notably evaluative beliefs (he calls them dispositions of evaluation) and beliefs that something is a reason for doing a certain kind of thing.

He then makes a preliminary characterization of an individual's reasons for acting. A reason for doing a particular act is a reason for some individual to do it just in case it satisfies an element of his motivation set. Then comes the first modification. If the reason satisfies an element of the individual's motivation set that is based on a false belief, it is not a reason for him to act in the relevant way. That is, I can think I have a reason for doing something even when I don't.

Equally important, I can have a reason for doing something even when I think I don't. For one thing, I may be ignorant of certain elements of my motivation set. For another (and this requires the second modification), my motivation set is not, Williams emphasizes, "statically given." Serious reflection on the elements of our motivation sets (Williams calls it rational deliberation from our motivation sets) can bring about new dispositions—new desires, new appreciations, new loyalties. Most people contemplating marriage or divorce, for example, find that they have all sorts of surprising reasons to choose one way or the other. They find themselves newly appreciative of certain traits of their lovers or spouses, newly apprehensive about others, newly attached to certain features of the single or married life, newly put off by others. To limit an individual's reasons to those that satisfy the elements of his motivation set before such reflection is to limit them unjustifiably.

But not to do so creates another problem. A reason for me to act is now one that satisfies a current element of my motivation set (or, more rightly, a current element not based on a false belief) or an element I would have upon serious reflection (and which would not be based on a false belief). And the "would" introduces a good deal of vagueness into the matter. Although I'm confident that no amount of reflection will result in the discovery that making the Buddha happy gives me a reason to do anything whatever, my confidence quickly wanes for other possibilities. Who knows how many of my wife's qualities I would find endearing upon reflection, and how many reasons for staying with her that gives me?

Williams isn't bothered by the vagueness, and there's no reason why he should be. Artificial precision is no virtue. Still, when we understand the internalist position this way, it begins to look as though *everybody* must have *some* reason to follow moral rules. Can we imagine someone with such a constricted motivation set that no amount of deliberation would give him the slightest reason to take Baier's moral point of view?

Think what we are asked to imagine—someone with no capacity for sympathy or empathy, someone with no concern for others, someone with no identification with any human community, someone with no sense of fairness. We are not asked to imagine the ordinary egoist, somebody who understands that he has some reason to follow moral rules but believes that he has better reason not to follow them. Nor are we asked to imagine someone who believes he has no reason to follow them but has never subjected his belief to serious reflection. What we are asked to imagine is a truly colossal failure of socialization—someone who has no disposition that can be satisfied by following moral rules, and who, even after serious reflection, would still not have one. (I am not, of course, including among the relevant dispositions such purely egoistic ones as the desire to impress a potential sexual conquest.)

Such a person must be either autistic or a Martian. Indeed, the more one thinks about it, the more one is struck by the thought that Harman's choice of Martians as his example of intelligent beings with no reason to treat us in a moral way was inevitable. (Not quite. Elsewhere, he picks Hitler, who seems as unlike the rest of us as a Martian.)[4]

THAT, AT ANY RATE, IS ONE WAY of looking at the matter. I'm not sure, though, that it's Williams's way. Consider his example of Owen Wingrave. As Williams tells the tale, Owen's parents believe that he should join the Army in order to uphold family honor. But Owen, who hates everything about military life, has no motivation whatever to enlist. Moreover, no amount of reflection on the elements of his motivation set will lead to his being so motivated. He has, Williams tells us, no reason to join.

I find it very puzzling that Williams reaches that conclusion without telling us much more about Owen. Does he have *no* concern for family honor? *No* concern to please his parents? (The list of such questions can go on indefinitely. Does he, for example, have no liking for travel? No liking for having others cook for him?) If not, then there are at least two elements of his motivation set that would be satisfied by his joining the Army. And that means, on Williams's account, that he does have reason to join the Army—not good enough to override his hatred of the Army, but reason just the same. Nothing in Williams's account requires that an individual's reason be a decisive one, or even a good one. He even makes that point explicit. So why does he stop after telling us that Owen hates the Army so much that nothing can motivate him to join, as though that were the only relevant fact about Owen?

Here's one possible answer. Perhaps Owen does have a desire to please his parents but does not believe that pleasing his parents is reason to do something he finds as loathsome as joining the Army. Or, to take a slightly different view of the matter, perhaps he has a *general* desire to please them but no desire to please them in this instance, and because of that he believes he has no reason to join the Army.

But if that is why *Williams* believes that Owen has no reason to join the Army, some change in his account of reasons is required. Instead of talking about *satisfaction* of the elements of an individual's motivation set, he must say something like the following. A reason for doing a particular thing is an individual's reason for doing it just in case reflection on the elements of his motivation set can lead him to the *belief* that it is a reason for him to do it.

There is, I think, something intuitively right about that. Fresh air and exercise generally give me good reason to take a walk, but do they give me any reason to go to Beirut to take a walk? Or, to pick a less fanciful example, loyalty to the state may have given Socrates good reason to do all sorts of things, but if he had decided that it gave him no reason to drink hemlock, would we want to disagree with him?

But there is also something intuitively wrong with the newly modified account. Take two people, each with the same relevant dispositions—Socrates and Pocrates, say. Socrates believes that loyalty to the state gives him no reason to drink his hemlock. Pocrates believes that it gives him some reason, but not a very good one.

Reasons

Does Pocrates have a reason to drink hemlock but Socrates not? Is there any real difference between the two except that they prefer different ways of talking?

I DON'T KNOW HOW TO ANSWER that question. I suspect that nobody does. The line between something being a poor reason for me to act and it being no reason for me to act seems incurably fuzzy. But before leaving it at that, let's take a look at the matter in relation to the central issue—reasons provided by moral rules.

We're talking to an egoist, trying to convince him that Baier is right. He agrees that cooperation is a good thing. He also agrees that cooperation requires trust, that moral rules provide the basis of that trust, and that it is therefore a good thing that most people behave according to moral rules. Moreover, he agrees that anybody who takes advantage of the good that comes from other people's following the rules but does not follow them himself is being unfair, so fairness, insofar as it leads to all those other good things, is itself a good thing.

So, we ask him, why doesn't he do the fair thing and follow moral rules? Because, he answers, none of that gives *him* any reason to follow moral rules. *His* only interest is to reap the benefits of all those good things. He has absolutely no interest in being fair himself.

On the newly modified account of reasons, we would have to agree with him. Although he is sincerely disposed to say some very nice things about fairness, cooperation and trustworthiness (he's certainly no Martian), he is no more disposed to be fair than Owen is to join the Army. He might, of course, cooperate when he cannot reap the benefits without cooperating, but that has nothing to do with anything but his own self-interest.

Now take another egoist who is just as agreeable as the first—

even more so, because she responds to our final question somewhat differently. She acknowledges that her high opinion of fairness, trustworthiness and cooperation gives her *some* reason for following the rules, but, all things considered, not much of one. Compared to her own self-interest, she says, it looks downright piddling.

On the newly modified account of reasons, we would have to agree with the second egoist as well as the first. Of course, we would also have to agree with her on Williams's account. But, at least when taking that account at face value, we would have to *disagree* with the first.

OUR TWO EGOISTS ARE very much like Socrates and Pocrates. And if we ask about the egoists what we asked about the hemlock refusers, my answer is the same. I don't know, and I suspect that nobody does. In fact, what I really suspect is that there is no answer to be known, which is just another way of saying that the line between a poor reason and no reason is incurably fuzzy. Sometimes we take reasons seriously, sometimes we dismiss them. Do we ever bother to ask ourselves whether we're dismissing a terrible reason rather than a nonreason? I don't. Nor do I think that any artificial precision will do us any good here. If somebody responds to the suggestion that she consider some reason with a dismissive "What kind of reason is that?" it makes no difference whether we answer "A rotten one" or "No reason at all."

So I won't try to choose between Williams's account of reasons, taken at face value, and what I've been calling the newly modified account. Whichever we choose, the egoist (or at least some egoists) remains rational. And the rest of us, nonegoists, do not necessarily act contrary to reason if we do not do what one ought to do.

To say that the egoist is rational is not, of course, to say that he is moral. And because my chief concern in this book is moral freedom, not intellectual freedom, I'd just as soon be done with him. He made his appearance here for one reason only—to allow us to see whether an adequate understanding of practical reason requires us to restrict moral freedom as much as Baier and others would like us to. It doesn't.

So let's get back to somebody like our reformed Butch Cassidy, somebody who does not think that the question "What's the best thing for me to do?" is just another way of asking "What best promotes my own self-interest?" Let's get back to somebody with a considered view of the good life, with personal values, ideals, and projects that give his life meaning and worth, somebody who thinks that the best thing for him to do is intimately connected with *them*, rather than with mere self-interest. And let's ask about him the question that ended Chapter 1. Does anybody or anything have any moral authority over how he leads *his* life?

That question can be put in the form of two challenges, one more daring than the other. The less daring one comes from Williams, who asks us to consider somebody whose view of the good life includes following moral rules but finds himself in a situation where to do so would be to sacrifice his ground project.[5] The sort of person envisioned by Williams knows that if he decides to pursue his ground project, he will cause harm of one kind or another to other people. He knows that and he cares about that. He also knows that he will never be able fully to justify himself to them, that they will always have a legitimate grievance against him. As an example, he offers a morally sensitive Gauguin, responsive to the demands of the impersonal point of view—most notably, his obligations to his family—as well as his own very personal reasons for going to Tahiti to paint.

To those who claim that the demands of impersonal morality

come first, Williams says the following.[6] Life must have substance if anything—including the demands of impersonal morality—is to make sense. But if life is to have substance, the demands of the impersonal point of view cannot override the personal point of view. Individuals must be morally free to weigh their ground projects against their obligations to others and to make their choices from the personal point of view. To demand otherwise from them is to demand that they live without meaning and self-worth.

THE MORE DARING CHALLENGE comes from Nietzsche.[7] What is the purpose of moral rules? The preservation and advancement of humanity. But preservation in what form? Advancement toward what end? In a form and toward an end determined by some group's conception of the good. But what if *my* conception of the good is radically different from that group's conception of the good? Why should I act in accordance with *its* conception instead of my own?

Both are challenges to the hegemony of moral rules. Externalist arguments attempt to establish that hegemony, but, I have argued, they fail. That leaves both challenges unmet.

What makes Williams's challenge the less daring of the two is this: It does not suggest that we read the impersonal point of view out of morality, but suggests only that we question its ultimate authority. It denies that only another obligation can override an obligation. It affirms instead that personal ideals can override an obligation. Nietzsche's challenge, on the other hand, suggests (at least on one reading of Nietzsche) that the impersonal point of view can and should be read out of morality, at least for individuals who have a considered view of the good life and the courage and strength to live accordingly.

Put another way, Nietzsche's challenge asks us to consider our second truism in its strongest form. To say that morality is a matter of individual choice is to say that acting according to his own conception of the good and only his own conception of the good is a morally legitimate option for any individual, and that his moral life is not thereby diminished but may be enhanced—despite my facile assertion of the contrary in Chapter 2.

Williams's challenge asks us to consider a somewhat weaker version of the second truism. To say that morality is a matter of individual choice is to say that impersonal morality *does* have claims on us, but it is also to say that it is up to the individual to balance those claims against his own projects.

Once again, these challenges survive externalist arguments. If they survive others, we'll have to return to my facile assertion of Chapter 2 and see whether we have better justification for accepting one or the other of the two just mentioned versions of the second truism. If it survives careful consideration, the weaker fares better than the stronger. If it doesn't, the stronger (indeed the strong*est*) fares better.

But first we have to consider our third truism more carefully. If some things are wrong regardless of what any society or individual has to say, then even the weaker version of the second truism must be further weakened. That is the subject of the next two chapters.

4

ABSOLUTE WRONGS

A FEW YEARS AGO I read a newspaper account of a photographer on a picnic with his lover. Somehow or other she fell victim to poison. According to the prosecutors, the photographer poisoned her. According to the photographer, he did not. But about one matter there was no disagreement. As she went into her death throes, the photographer gave no assistance. Instead, he took out his camera and started to shoot. She died in agony while he went after his masterwork—a documentary record of each stage of her final minutes.

I don't know whether the film was ever developed or whether the images were ever printed. Nor do I know the outcome of the trial. Nor do I remember what city or what country it all happened in. But I do remember thinking that I could not imagine the incredible awfulness of realizing that you're going to die and that somebody you love probably poisoned you and in any case would rather film your death than prevent it or at least take you in his arms and comfort you.

And I think I know this: What that photographer did is wrong regardless of what any society or individual has to say about it. (I think I know it even if he didn't poison her, but from now on I'll assume that he did.)

I say "think I know" because it is a very strange thing to know, and what makes it a very strange thing to know is that if I really do know it I don't know how I know it. I know that what he did is forbidden by the moral rules of my society and any other society that comes readily to mind. I know that it is beyond the bounds of my morality and the morality of anyone else I would let live among the rest of us. I also know that the only printable words I can think of to describe a person who thinks it within the bounds of his morality are "depraved," "demented," "inhuman," and the like. And I know *how* I know all those things. But how do I know that what he did is wrong regardless of what any society or individual—including me and including the photographer himself—has to say about it?

THE SHORT ANSWER, of course, is this: I just know it. It is the sort of answer that most ordinary people (nonphilosophers) would give. It is also the sort of answer that some philosophers (most notably, David Ross) did give. And I like that answer. Like most people (philosophers and nonphilosophers alike), in my ordinary life I'm an intuitionist. But I've been a philosopher long enough to know that the answer is a philosophical nonstarter.

The utilitarian answer is also a nonstarter. For one thing, I certainly do not know that utilitarianism is true. For another, I won't even listen to the utilitarian answer, because I do know that I can imagine an aftermath of the picnic so optimific that a consistent utilitarian would have to say that what the photographer did was not wrong. And that is something I will not accept.

The answer of the impartial observer theorist, even though it seems to be making a comeback, is another answer that I take to be a nonstarter. I can imagine all sorts of impartial observers, some who think like me and some who don't. If *the* impartial observer doesn't—if she should turn out to be a utilitarian, say—then I have no interest in what she has to say about the matter.

What about the social contract theorist's answer? If it is nothing more than the obvious point that society's rules forbid what the photographer did, it, too, is a nonstarter. What I think I know is that what the photographer did is wrong regardless of what any society has to say. But most social contract theorists have a more sophisticated answer than that. The relevant fact is not that his society's rules forbid what he did, but that the rules of any society must forbid it if they are to be valid moral rules. That answer is a better one, but after Chapter 3 it, too, is a nonstarter. It does not meet Nietzsche's challenge.

Well, not exactly a nonstarter. If we ask such social contract theorists why the rules of any society must forbid what the photographer did if they are to be valid moral rules, we get a Kantian answer. So let's forget about society's rules and go directly to Kant. Why is what the photographer did wrong? Because if ever there was a perfect example of one person using another person merely as a means to his own ends, this is it.

But how do I know *that*? How do I know that a perfect example of a violation of Kant's famous dictum is wrong regardless of what any society or individual has to say about it? What I'd like to say but obviously can't say is this: I just do.

KANT ARRIVED AT HIS FAMOUS dictum through a variety of paths. Many we cannot take, either because they begin with assumptions already ruled out in earlier chapters, or because they take us through metaphysical positions that have lost credibility throughout the years. We cannot, for example, follow a path that takes us through noumenal selves, because there are no such things. Nor can we follow a path that begins with a conceptual analysis of duty or moral law, because, however astute Kant's analyses may be, the challenge posed by Nietzsche rules that out. We are not asking what duty requires, but why the moral life requires us to do what duty requires rather than what is in accordance with our own conceptions of the good. For the same reason, we cannot follow a path that includes the claim that the purpose of reason is to produce a will good in itself, not happiness. Nor, for the same reason, can we follow a path that takes us through a distinction between the cognitive task (pure reason) and the executive task.

Fortunately, there are a few paths we can take, or at least begin on. They are, perhaps, the most direct of all. Each one begins with Kant's conception of a person, but we need not call it Kant's conception. It is one that has held up very well. Whatever else we may want to say about persons (that they need or need not be embodied, for example), persons are rational agents. They act on reasons.

But there is more to the matter than that. Persons do not just *act* on reasons. They *know* that they do. They are aware of themselves as beings who reason and act on reason and are thereby able to engage in second-order reasoning. That is, they are able to reason about their own reasoning. And that allows them to evaluate their reasons, to subject their desires and goals to rational scrutiny, and to acquire second-order beliefs and desires.

To put all this in Kantian terms, persons are autonomous beings. To put it in decidedly non-Kantian terms, persons are beings who can take what Daniel Dennett calls the intentional stance toward themselves.[1] The intentional stance is one of three stances we can take toward any creature capable of complex behavior. To view a creature's behavior as the product of physical laws is to take what Dennett calls the physical stance toward it. To view its behavior as the product of an evolutionary solution to a problem of adaptation is to take what he calls the design stance. And to view its behavior as the product of intentional attitudes (beliefs, desires, motivations, and the like) is to take the intentional stance. We can—and often do—take the intentional stance toward our pets, but they are not persons. They cannot take the intentional stance toward themselves. We, of course, can—and do—take the intentional stance toward ourselves, so we are persons.

THIS CONCEPTION OF THE PERSON is, I take it, as uncontroversial as any philosophical conception can get. So let's begin along the first path that leads from it. But first, let me give one caveat. These paths are abstractions from the *Groundwork*, not an exercise in Kant scholarship. I make no claim that they are Kant's actual arguments, but only that they are very Kantian. They are, I think, a way of reconstructing what remains of his arguments after the offending assumptions have been removed. How well they work is something I'll consider after we look at all of them.

Ordinary practical reasoning (Aristotelian practical reasoning) is means-end reasoning. Whatever gets me what I want has some worth for me. The issue of the worth of the ends does not arise. Ordinarily, that issue arises only when I think of the end as a means to some further end.

In that case, what I take to have worth is ordinarily something I take to have only relative worth—worth as a means to some end. Of course, there are some ends that I desire intrinsically, rather than as means to some further ends, but even those are not of absolute worth. Their worth is relative to my intrinsic desires. As those change, so do my judgments of worth.

If anything is to have absolute worth, it must have worth independent of any particular ends and any particular desires. And that kind of worth belongs to my autonomy—because my autonomy is what allows me to evaluate my motivations and patterns of reasoning in light of *whatever* intrinsic desires I might have, to change them if necessary, and to act accordingly. Moreover, the same holds for all persons. Their autonomy must be of absolute worth to them. Therefore, I should not interfere with any person's autonomy. That is, I should not use anybody merely as a means to my own end.

THE SECOND PATH is a variation of the first. When I engage in second-order reasoning, when I step back and evaluate my motivations, I am taking a critical look at them. I am subjecting them to rational scrutiny according to some norms of rationality. If I am to subject *all* of them to rational scrutiny, or if I am to subject anyone to rational scrutiny in a way that does not itself require rational scrutiny, I must see these norms as being not just *my* norms, but the norms that *any* rational agent must follow. That is, I must abstract from myself as scrutinizer everything but my own autonomy. All my desires, inclinations, motivations, and projects belong only to what I am scrutinizing.

When I scrutinize my motivations in this way, I am not just *recognizing* relative worth, as I do in ordinary practical reasoning. In the latter case, the judgment that something has worth automatically follows the judgment that it is the means to something I desire. But in the kind of scrutiny I'm concerned with here, something else is going on. I am, as an autonomous agent, deciding what *ought* to have worth for me. I am *conferring* worth through the exercise of my autonomy. And that makes autonomy of absolute worth—because it confers worth on ends, rather than receiving worth from them. Not just my autonomy—any person's autonomy. The rational norms I apply are those of all autonomous beings, and the autonomous *I* who evaluates my motivations is indistinguishable from any autonomous *I*. Autonomy itself is of absolute worth.

So, since autonomy alone is of absolute worth, I should not interfere with any person's autonomy. That is, I should not use anybody merely as a means to my own ends.

WHAT MAKES THE SECOND PATH a variation of the first is that it relies on the notion of absolute worth and argues that autonomy is what has it. The third path does neither. It is, however, a variation of the second. It, too, relies on the notion of rational norms that any rational agent must apply.

When I scrutinize my motivations according to such norms, I must recognize that anybody else scrutinizing her own motivations must get the same results as I do, since she is applying the same norms. In that case, my evaluations must apply not only to me but to all autonomous beings. Whatever motivations survive must survive for all autonomous beings. Whatever motivations do not survive cannot survive for any autonomous being. One way of putting that point is this: When I evaluate my motivations, I am acting as an autonomous being legislating for a republic of autonomous beings.

Such a republic is what Williams calls a *notional* republic.[2] That is, it is a republic whose laws are not enforced with sanctions, but are freely chosen by its autonomous members. Autonomous beings will not choose laws that interfere with their autonomy. So I should not interfere with any person's autonomy. That is, I should not use anybody merely as a means to my own ends.

Absolute Wrongs

THESE THREE PATHS ARE, again, abstractions from the *Groundwork*. They are also very short. An even shorter way of putting them is this: If we understand ourselves and others as persons, we must also respect ourselves and others as persons. Here's an even shorter way: The notion of a person is the notion of someone who commands respect.

What is most interesting about them is that they arrive at their Kantian conclusion from the *inside*. They do not begin from the impersonal point of view, but from the personal one. Indeed, another way of putting them is this: Anyone who fully reflects on her subjective motivation set and fully understands what she is doing when she does that will be led to Kantian respect. And that's why I can say that some things are wrong regardless of what any society or individual has to say about them. Because anybody who says otherwise has not fully reflected on her motivation set or does not fully understand what she did in doing so. And if that's right, the Nietzschean challenge has been met. Or has it?

I ask that question because the arguments, even though they begin from the personal point of view, do not end there. They end at the impersonal point of view. This is most explicit in the third argument, which takes us through a notional republic of autonomous beings. In thinking of myself as a legislator in that republic, I put myself in the position of being a maker and follower of rules. But once I know what the rules of some notional republic require, why can't I ask myself whether the best thing for me to do is to follow them?

Let me put the matter another way. Let's grant that the notion of a person is the notion of someone who commands respect. Let's grant also that anyone who fully reflects on her motivation set and fully understands what she's doing when she does that will be led to Kantian respect. But all that gives her is an element of her motivation set, respect for persons. Now that is certainly something, but it is not enough to get to Kant's real conclusion—that respect for persons is overriding. To get there, we need his notional republic, or something like it. At the least, we must see respect for persons as being more than just a motivation. We must see it as embodying a law. That is, we must see ourselves as being in the legislation business.

But why should we see ourselves that way? Kant has an answer to that question, and it involves his conception of autonomy, which is not quite the conception I began with. Kant's conception of autonomy cannot be divorced from legislation. To him, an autonomous agent is someone who is her own legislator. She does not just act on reasons, but according to rules that she issues to herself. She follows imperatives, some hypothetical, those relative to her inclinations, and one categorical, the one that is not. And that is what makes it categorical—that it is not relative to her inclinations. It is the one she issues as an autonomous being, period.

The conception of autonomy I began with makes no mention of legislation, rules, or imperatives. My autonomous person is someone who acts according to reasons that she is capable of weighing and evaluating, someone who is capable of taking the intentional stance toward herself. That was, of course, deliberate. To begin with imperatives and the like is to burke Nietzsche's challenge altogether. Nietzsche was not in the business of legislating, and he did not want to be. His transvaluation of value was intended not just as a transition from weakness to strength, from pity to generosity of spirit, from slavishness to nobility. It was intended also as a transition from imperatives to dispositions, from rules to character, from obligations to personal projects.

If a Kantian argument is to meet Nietzsche's challenge, then, it cannot begin with Kant's conception of autonomy, but with a conception like the one I began with. But even then, it fails.

Absolute Wrongs

STILL, THERE IS SOMETHING seductive about such arguments. The idea that recognizing the importance of my own autonomy requires me to recognize the importance of the autonomy of others and the related idea that self-respect is intimately connected to respect for persons both seem profoundly right. It is extremely difficult to imagine someone who respects herself but has absolutely no respect for anybody else.

But we don't need Kantian arguments to get us there. We can get there by certain considerations from Chapter 2. To have ground projects, I said there, to be able to answer the question why we should go on, presupposes some identification with the members of some community and its values. So my own sense of worth, my own self-respect, is tied to my sense that others have worth, that others command respect.

But when we look at the matter that way, a crucial part of our Kantian arguments dissolves. What is key to my sense of worth are my ground projects, not my autonomy. Of course, only an autonomous being can have ground projects (or any projects at all), but that is beside the point. Nobody answers the question "Why go on?" with "Because I'm an autonomous being." Indeed, to conceive of ourselves merely as autonomous beings is much more likely to bring on a sense of vertigo (as Sartre was fond of stressing) than respect.[3]

I go on because of my projects, not my autonomy. And my sense of self-worth is closely tied to what I do, not what I am, if "what I am" is just my autonomy. As Sartre would put it, my autonomy is nothing but—well, nothing but nothingness. And I, as *just* an autonomous being, am a hole in being, which I try to fill with my projects. If we take the talk of nothingness and holes metaphorically, the point seems well taken. (So, for that matter, does another point of Sartre's. Even if our autonomy is the source of our values, that

68

doesn't mean that we value *it*. We are as likely to attempt to flee it in bad faith as to take joy in it.)

If our projects are what really matter to us, then reason easily leads us to the conclusion that other people's projects are what really matter to *them*. But reason does not so easily lead us to the conclusion that other people's projects must matter to *us*. Whether they do and how much they do depends not only on reason but also on our own beliefs, values, dispositions and projects.

Of course, the same can be said of autonomy. If my autonomy is what really matters to me, then reason easily leads me to the conclusion that other people's autonomy really matters to them, not to the conclusion that it must really matter to me. And that is because the autonomous *I* who evaluates my motivations is *not* abstracted from them. When I evaluate some particular motivation, I do so as someone who brackets only that one. The rest remain, and they, not some norms of reason that any rational agent must apply, are my guides.

I am like Otto Neurath's famous boat repairer, who, in his boat out on the water, requires the stability of the other planks as he replaces one of them.[4] To Neurath, each plank was a belief, and the point of his metaphor was that we have no position outside our belief system from which to evaluate any one belief. My boat repairer has no position outside his belief and motivation system from which to evaluate any one motivation. He is also a practical reasoner much like Harman's. Or Williams's.

STEPHEN DARWALL THINKS OTHERWISE.[5] At least, he thinks it possible to step outside that system. He also thinks that whatever anybody outside that system would choose is the best thing to choose.

To be outside that system is to be behind what he calls a *thick veil of ignorance*. What makes it thick is that it precludes all knowledge of any particularly human motivation, including my own, and all influence of any particularly human motivation, including my own. Someone behind his thick veil is allowed to know and be influenced by only what will be known by and influence any arbitrary (not necessarily human) rational agent. What that makes such a person, of course, is a Kantian legislator.

What makes his approach worth looking at now is that it, like the Kantian paths discussed above, begins from the inside. He first announces himself as a Humean internalist and then emerges with the Kantian legislator. The route is not a continuous one, though. It is rather like Baier's. Baier, remember, has no quarrel with internalism as an account of practical reasoning's explanatory aspect, but rejects it as an account of practical reasoning's normative one. Darwall is more subtle on this matter. After presenting his Humean view of reasons, he goes on to discuss the normative aspect of practical reasoning and then to reconcile the results with his initial internalist account. If he succeeds, Kant is saved.

HIS INTERNALIST ACCOUNT is as much like Williams's as Hume's. Many kinds of dispositions, not just desires, are relevant in determining what makes something a reason for some individual to act. Rational deliberation from these dispositions is also relevant, rational deliberation including vivid imagining of all the relevant facts and dispassionate consideration of them. Moreover, what makes some reasons weightier than others is that the agent would take them to be so after the same kind of reasoning.

Although it is possible to nitpick about some of the details, the account in its general outline should be acceptable to most internalists. At any rate, it is to me. Once we consider the normative aspect of reasoning, though, the account requires some modification. After all, some people are better reasoners than others, and some ways of reasoning are better than others. (To take an epistemic analogy, some people come closer to maximizing explanatory coherence than others, and some inductive rules are better than others.) To recognize that is to recognize the existence of some rational normative system. It is also to recognize oneself as a member of that system who is motivated to adhere to that system. (To return to the epistemic analogy, I accept explanatory coherence as a cognitive virtue and some inductive rules as better able than others to achieve it, and I am motivated to use those rules to achieve it.) And to recognize that is to recognize that these norms cannot require of me what they do not require of any other member of this system, and to be motivated to adhere to that system is to be motivated to do what is required of any member of that system.

But if we now ask what such a system requires, we are not asking what it requires of me. We are asking what it requires of *any* rational agent. That is, we must place ourselves behind the thick veil of ignorance.

IS THE KANTIAN LEGISLATOR SAVED? No. The reason he's not can be found in the last two sentences of the argument. The rational norms that apply to everybody apply to every real flesh and blood person, with real commitments, values, and projects. And how they apply is, at least in part, determined by those real commitments, values, and projects. To say that they apply to everybody is not to say that they apply to some abstract nobody—to a Sartrean hole in being, if I may repeat a metaphor that is becoming more and more appealing to me. It is to say that they apply to every *body*. This is, of course, merely to repeat what I said in Chapter 3. There is no reason to believe that a rational normative system requires of every individual the same outcome independent of his motivation set. To repeat the question I asked there: Why isn't the norm of achieving explanatory coherence and satisfying intrinsic desire absolute enough? Also to repeat: It will do no good to draw an analogy to epistemic reasoning.

What follows, on the other hand, is not to repeat: A Kantian legislator is as unlike you and me as Harman's Martians are unlike you and me. Nothing *matters* to him. Why should his only reasons for acting be my best reasons for acting? They leave out everything that matters to me. Don't my deepest concerns make any relevant difference? And if they don't, why should I care what this legislator says?

This *is* to repeat: A life must have substance if anything is to make sense. That is Williams's challenge.

I SHOULD PROBABLY BE HAPPIER to get back to that point than I am. It reinforces the conclusions of Chapter 3. The problem is that I think I know that what the photographer did is wrong regardless of what any society or individual has to say but I don't know how I know it if I do know it.

But perhaps I was asking too much. What I was looking for was a solution to Nietzsche's challenge, an argument showing that individuals do not have the moral freedom to violate at least some demands of the impersonal point of view. What I was looking for was the strongest possible reading of our third truism. A weaker reading may be available. If we lower our sights a bit, it may be sufficient.

When deciding the best thing for me to do I am not, I said, in the legislating business. But that doesn't mean that I'm never in the legislating business. Moral rules are society's rules, and I've been expressing that point by saying that moral rules are the product of a social contract. Now I'd like to add this: As participants in the social contract, we are all in the legislating business. The rules we agree on are the rules we expect everyone to follow, and whether we expect them to be overriding in every case or not, we certainly expect them to be given high priority. Moreover, we expect people to follow them without fear of sanctions. Although we have laws backed by the full power of the state to support some of them, and although we have more informal sanctions to support the rest, we still expect that most people will follow them merely because they think they should. Put another way, if criminal and civil laws are laws of a political republic, moral rules are rules of a notional one.

Can we go on to say that moral rules cannot be valid rules if they violate Kantian respect? Many philosophers have gone on to say that, or at least something like it—that, of course, is what led us to Kant—and it does seem to be a natural step. The considerations of the previous paragraph naturally lead to the view that to be valid, society's rules must be rules that all members of society would freely agree on as rules to guide the behavior of everyone. That is, to be valid, they must be acceptable to all members who take the impersonal point of view.

OF COURSE, THAT DOES NOT get us very far. For one thing, there is no *one* way of taking the impersonal point of view. Depending on how many gradations of thickness we can imagine, there are that many veils of ignorance, and each one picks out a different way of taking the impersonal point of view.

For another, there is the problem of conditioning. However thick the veil, whatever the individuals behind it will agree to must reflect their conceptions of the good, Kant and Darwall not withstanding. Can we imagine real flesh and blood people agreeing on rules that do not reflect what they have already been conditioned to value? (Just think of the varying roles that honor has played from culture to culture, or obedience, or individualism.) And if we can't—I certainly can't—what happens to the requirement that the rules be freely chosen?

And, finally, there are the problems of bad choosers, bad negotiators, the obstinate, the unimaginative, the stupid, the unconcerned, and a variety of other suspect types. Should their role be as prominent as everybody else's? Indeed, why should we bother listening to them at all?

The standard move at this point is to impose what Paul Taylor calls the ideal mutual acknowledgment test.[6] Valid moral rules are those that autonomous agents would agree on under ideal conditions of freedom, rationality and factual knowledge. But I don't know what those ideal conditions are. Neither, for that matter, does Taylor, who admits that his view leaves us in the position of not knowing whether our moral rules are valid.

Taylor doesn't see anything wrong with finding himself in that position, but I certainly do. To say that a moral rule is valid is to say, from the impersonal point of view, that it creates a real obligation. It is to say that one ought to do what the rule requires (which is not, of course, necessarily the same as saying that the best thing for me to do is follow the rule on any given occasion). Now, suppose that under ideal conditions autonomous agents would decide on rules that forbid private property. In that case, many of our moral rules are invalid, which means that I have no obligation to pay my debts. Surely, we must make some concessions to the historical circumstances we now find ourselves in, however *non*ideal. Surely, we must recognize that a system of moral rules can fall short of the ideal—whatever that may be—and still be valid, still generate real obligations.

The better course, then, is to save ideal conditions as a possible test for the *best* system of moral rules and accept something less as a test for *valid* moral rules. So let us begin with real people, in their real historical circumstances, with their own conceptions of the good, and let's take valid moral rules to be those that are freely agreed on by the individuals who are willing to take the impersonal point of view.

TO ACCEPT THAT ACCOUNT is to adopt the spirit of relativism. What people freely agree to varies with historical circumstances and with shared and individual conceptions of the good. But to admit that different societies can have different valid moral rules is not to admit that all systems of moral rules are equal. With increased knowledge, say, there might come better rules. Indeed, there often have come better rules. (What makes some rules better than others is a matter I'll deal with in a later chapter.)

How generous a spirit of relativism we adopt depends on how we interpret the condition that the rules be freely accepted. In most cases, the acceptance of moral rules is the product of conditioning. That is, we are socialized into the social contract. And given that obvious fact, it is hard to say that most people freely adopt them.

Absolute Wrongs

Did women in prefeminist days, for instance, conditioned as children to obey their future husbands, freely choose the rule that they ought to obey their husbands? Did they freely choose the rule that mothers of young children ought not work unless necessity demanded it?

These are difficult questions, and I'm not sure how to answer them. Whether conditioning counts as education or social coercion is an extremely ideological matter. Feminists see the grade school readers of earlier times as sexist and coercive. Traditionalists see them as providing appropriate moral education, but see today's readers as coercive. Feminists, of course, see them as liberating.

Such problems no doubt provide one motivation for philosophers like Taylor to require that rules be mutually acceptable under ideal conditions of freedom. And the problems are serious enough that I almost wish I could join them. But only almost. The reason I can't is that the only sense I can make out of ideal conditions of freedom are those that rule out all conditioning—and those are impossible conditions. They are not only impossible to bring about, but they are impossible to imagine. Who knows what someone with no moral conditioning would find acceptable?

The best thing to do, then, is to interpret "freely chosen" broadly. Within any society, it is possible to distinguish, according to that society's beliefs, coercive and noncoercive measures—allowing, of course, for significant gray areas. In prefeminists days, readers picturing women as mothers and housewives but men as workers in the outside world were not considered coercive. They were considered reflections of the normal home lives of school children and expressions of a widely shared conception of the way things ought to be. Certainly, they were seen as no more coercive than books portraying honesty and loyalty as virtues. However much they offend our sensibilities today, however wrong we take them to be now, according to the moral sensibilities of the day they were no more coercive than any other moral education. So we should, I think, consider the rules in question as freely chosen as any others.

The same cannot, however, be said for the rules concerning the proper place of blacks. To the extent that blacks acquiesced to them, they did so out of fear or resignation. They knew the dangers of being "uppity." But to acquiesce in fear of threatened sanctions is not to agree freely. The rules about the proper place of blacks were not valid, then, unlike the rules about the proper place of mothers with young children. Mothers of young children did have an obligation to stay home with them, but blacks did not have an obligation to be servile to whites.

Lest this result seem harsh or sexist, let me quickly make two very important points. First, to say that a rule is valid is not to *endorse* it. I'm glad that mothers of young children no longer have those obligations. I think that the changes in the rules we've seen in the last decades are good changes, changes that made for a better shared morality. (Again, I'll deal with the question of what makes some moralities better than others in a later chapter.)

Second, to say that a rule is valid is *not* to say that the best thing for any individual to do is to follow it, and to say that someone has an obligation to do something is not to say that the best thing for that person to do is to fulfill it. A judgment that I have an obligation to do something is a judgment made from the impersonal point of view. We have yet to find a convincing argument that the impersonal point of view overrides the personal point of view, rationallly or morally.

So I CAN REMAIN THE DEFENDER of the rebellious feminist in pre-feminist times. What about the photographer?

There is at least one important difference between him and the

77

rebellious feminist. Leaving her young child with a babysitter while she worked may have been wrong according to the moral rules of her day, but it is not wrong according to the moral rules of our day. What the photographer did, on the other hand, was wrong regardless of what any society or individual has to say. And I know that because no valid system of moral rules could allow it. No system of rules that permits what the photographer did could be freely agreed upon.

Or could it? It all depends on how we interpret the phrase "what the photographer did." We could, I suppose, imagine some traditional society having some sort of freely agreed upon ritual including something like what he did that takes place on some special occasion or other, rather like that imagined in Shirley Jackson's story "The Lottery." We could also imagine, I suppose, some other traditional society freely agreeing to punish fornication by death and allowing some official artist to depict the death scene as a public warning to would-be fornicators.

What I can't imagine, though, is any society with freely agreed upon rules allowing any arbitrary individual to poison his lover without her consent and then photograph her death throes rather than help or comfort her. The problem is not just that there seems to be no point to the rule, nor even that it precludes the kind of trust that moral rules are intended to secure, nor even that it is extremely difficult to imagine any society wanting to encourage that kind of cruelty among intimates. More deeply, I can't imagine rational adult individuals freely agreeing that they may rightfully be put in the position of the lover without their consent just because someone like the photographer wants them in that position. And that, again, marks an important difference between what the photographer did and what the rebellious feminist in prefeminist times did.

But there may be an important similarity too. Let's suppose, as it is reasonable to do, that photography was as much his ground project as art was Matisse's. Let's also suppose something far less likely—that for years he'd been pondering the matter and had come to believe with much conviction that a series of shots of his lover in her death throes and only that would give his lifework and thus his life any value.

What we've just supposed is the severest test of Nietzsche's challenge. I know that what he did was wrong regardless of what any society or individual has to say about it, I know that the only printable words I can think of to describe him are "inhuman" and the like, and I know that I do not want him living among the rest of us. But I don't know that I can call what he did immoral (except, of course, from the impersonal point of view and my personal point of view). I don't know that because I still don't know that the moral life requires, at least sometimes, that the impersonal point of view override the personal.

WE'LL RETURN TO THE PHOTOGRAPHER in the final two chapters. There is much more to say about him. In this chapter, my concern was not him, but what he did. I wanted to show that what he did was wrong regardless of what any society or individual has to say.

First, I tried to reach that conclusion in its strongest interpretation. That is, I tried to conclude not just that what he did was absolutely wrong from the impersonal point of view, but absolutely immoral, period. I tried that by seeing if we could reach a Kantian conclusion from the inside—that is, as internalists. We couldn't.

But a weaker conclusion was available, and I took it. From the impersonal point of view, what the photographer did is wrong regardless of what any society or individual has to say. No valid system of moral rules could allow what he did.

Absolute Wrongs

There is, however, another place to look for the stronger conclusion. If there are absolute wrongs from the impersonal point of view, perhaps there are absolute bads from the personal one. That is, perhaps some conceptions of the good life cannot count as *moral* conceptions of the good life regardless of what any individual has to say. That is a conclusion I considered in Chapter 2 but failed to reach. But there might be another path toward it, and that is the subject of the next chapter.

5

GOOD LIVES

NO DOUBT ONE OF THE CHIEF REASONS that so few moral philosophers have discussed the good life is that it is very difficult to say anything about it that isn't achingly banal. No doubt another is the justified suspicion that there is no such thing as *the* good life, but only a variety of good lives. The two are, of course, related. The greater the variety of good lives, the less of substance to be said about them. And banality is a ready substitute for substance.

Aristotle had a great advantage on this score. Armed with a metaphysics that put telos at the heart of nature and supported by a culture that put virtues and the good ahead of rules and the right, he was able to provide a good deal of substance. But causality and Schroedinger's wave function have replaced teleology, and the culture of ancient Greece is not our own, so substance is a difficult thing to deliver.

It is, however, what we're looking for in this chapter. In particular, we are looking for a substantial conception of the good life that allows us to meet the challenges of Nietzsche and Williams. But first, we must rehearse some of the banalities.

To LIVE THE GOOD LIFE is to live according to one's conception of the good. That's a short way of putting the matter. Too short. It seems to leave nothing out. If we assume at least a rough equivalence between what we desire and what we take to be good and conjoin that assumption with folk psychology, we get the result that everybody whose desires are not routinely frustrated leads the good life. And we certainly want something meatier than that.

An obvious way to tighten the original characterization is to reintroduce the notion of a ground project. That introduces higher goods into our characterization, or at least more important goods. Our ground projects involve the goods that matter to us most, the ones that give us a sense of self-worth and our lives meaning and substance. To judge my life good I must judge it substantial. To judge it worth continuing I must judge it of worth. So the good life requires ground projects.

But that doesn't get us all that far. People without ground projects are people who write suicide notes. So, for that matter, are people whose ground projects are routinely frustrated. Both groups remind us that we need further tightening. Otherwise we include all non-suicides and many suicides.

The standard move at this point is to introduce the notion of practical wisdom. To live the good life, we must choose wisely. What it is to choose wisely, of course, depends on one's theory of practical wisdom, and such theories, like the theories of practical reason we looked at earlier, can be more or less ambitious. Let's begin with an unambitious one.

Someone with practical wisdom will have at least a fair idea of what matters to him and how much it matters to him. He will also have at least a fair idea of what he's good at and the sorts of things he enjoys doing. And he will be reflective enough to ask himself from time to time whether he's got things right. Among the things he will be most concerned to get right is what most matters to him.

Moreover, someone with practical wisdom will be pretty good at ordering his life. Allowing for an acceptable degree of backsliding, he won't let his ground projects slip away from him. Nor, for that matter, will he let them overwhelm him. He will, that is, have a sense of a full life as well as a meaningful one, and he will try to live both. He will also, with sufficient practical wisdom and a minimum amount of luck, be successful at it.

Two things have been left out of this extremely unambitious account—ideals and virtues. They do, however, have their respective places.

Consider ideals. The most important enter at two places. The first involves our ground projects. To pursue them is inevitably to pursue our most important ideals. That was the point of introducing Matisse and the immigrant tailor as examples of people pursuing ground projects.

The second place is a bit less obvious, because my remarks about practical wisdom included nothing about character. But someone with practical wisdom will certainly want and try to be a certain sort of person. Some of the character traits he will strive for will be specific to his projects—physical courage if he is a football running back, for example, or aesthetic sensibility if he's a poet—some will be necessary for the successful pursuit of any project—sufficient attentiveness and dedication, for example—and some will have nothing to do with his other projects but will be projects in them-

Good Lives

selves—compassion and dignity, say, if he is enough like you and
me. These are also his ideals.

They also give us a good start on his virtues. Whatever other
kinds of virtues there might be, these are among the most important—character traits necessary for the successful pursuit of our
projects and those we take to be necessary if we are to be successful
human beings.

It is tempting, given this account of virtues, to substitute "detrimental" for "necessary" and offer it as an account of the corresponding vices, but I don't think that will do. It would give us far
too many vices. Indeed, it would have the potential of turning any
virtue into a vice, on the reasonable assumption that pursuit of some
projects is detrimental to the successful pursuit of others. That is
why the good life requires some ordering. Moreover, to yield to the
temptation would be to strike a severe blow to inept hobbyists who
still derive pleasure from their hobbies, from the secret poetry writer
who knows nothing about poetry to the poker player who, after
being dealt the sixth card in a game of seven card stud, has to be
reminded that nothing is wild.

Put another way, vices are *somebody's* vices, and the mere fact
that Martina Navratilova and Jane Doe both play tennis does not
mean that inattentiveness to their backhand volleys evinces a vice
in both. Put still another way (the way John Atwell was kind enough
to put it to me one day), vices are self-burdens. They are dispositions
that interfere with the successful pursuit of the projects that matter
to us—most notably, our ground projects. They are the dispositions
that account for our backsliding, that damage our self-respect or
would damage it if we were to reflect upon them. They are com-
promises of our ideals, burdens that we carry in pursuit of the good
life. And to exercise practical wisdom is to exercise the know-how
to minimize their weight.

ALL OF THE ABOVE is, again, extremely unambitious. What makes it unambitious is that it is closely tied to an internalist account of practical reason, as, of course, it would have to be. It also manifests the suspicion that the good life is really a variety of good lives. And it does nothing to meet either Nietzsche's challenge or Williams's.

That last remark raises the chief concern of this chapter, but before pursuing it I should point out another feature of the foregoing that makes it unambitious. Although it says that a good life is an *ordered* life, it does not say that a good life is a *planned* life. Or, more to the point, whatever I did say about practical wisdom, I did not say that it involves the following of what John Rawls calls a rational life plan.[1]

To be sure, my remarks are consistent with Rawls's view of practical wisdom, but they are, when seen against it, incomplete. They leave out the perspectives of later selves who look back and judge the decisions of today's self. According to Rawls, practical wisdom requires us to think of our lives as wholes, spread out over time, with the perspective of each temporal slice given its full due. In that case, a life that ends in regret is a life unwisely lived.

By "regret" here, Rawls does not mean the mere wish that things had turned out otherwise. He means, rather, the sense that we'd made important mistakes—that we'd taken risks not worth taking, pursued projects not worth pursuing, made decisions we would not have made on further reflection. The sort of regret he intends includes self-reproach. And it is a requirement of practical wisdom that we do not make choices that end in regret.

Since Rawls adopts another principle he calls the Aristotelian Principle (which we'll look at later in this chapter), we may call this one his Second Aristotelian Principle. Practical wisdom aims toward eudaimonia, and a rational life plan ends in it. Rawls sees eudaimonia as being highly individualized—he, too, believes in good lives rather than the good life—but in another respect he sees it in a very Aristotelian way. If it's not there at the end of life, it never was there. Whether I have lived my good life depends on my judgment at the end. Why? Because a good life, as Aristotle also told us, is a rational life, and a rational life does not end in regret.

Given the obvious circularity in the first clause—in a post-Aristotelian age we keep an eye on the good life as we try to characterize practical wisdom—I see no reason to take exception to it. Nor do I see any reason to take exception to the second—as long as we add a *ceteris paribus* condition. Other things being equal, a life that does not end in regret *is* a better life than one that does. So, keeping an eye on the good life as I characterize practical wisdom, I can easily say that practical wisdom seeks to avoid regret. But I cannot so easily say that it always succeeds. A failure to avoid regret need not be a failure of practical wisdom. Someone may have succeeded in living a rational life but failed to live a completely good one. That is the point of the *ceteris paribus* condition.

Why add it? Because there are limits to what we can expect from practical wisdom, just as there are limits to what we can expect from epistemic wisdom. And Rawls, in presenting a more ambitious account of practical wisdom than I have chanced, may overstep them. It may be that we cannot give the perspectives of later selves their due, because we cannot know what those perspectives will be. In many of the most important dilemmas, perhaps the best that we can do is make a reasoned guess—and hope.

WILLIAMS PUTS THE MATTER THIS WAY: The perspective of deliberation is *from here*. The perspective of assessment with greater knowledge is *from there*. And we cannot know how our current decisions will affect that assessment. Whether we look back with regret or not is a matter of luck.[2]

In that case, we can put the ambitiousness of Rawls's view like this: It assumes that reason can protect us from a certain kind of dashed hope, that with sufficient reflection we can know now that if certain projects fail, our disappointment will not turn to bitterness and self-reproach, that we can know now the attitudes, feelings, and beliefs that will shape our final assessment of our lives and choices.

It also assumes that later selves will be right in their judgments, because they have greater knowledge than earlier ones. But this is one case where greater knowledge may mislead as easily as enlighten. Knowing how things have worked out, we may blame ourselves for not foreseeing what was in fact unforeseeable. It is, after all, as difficult to give the perspectives of past selves their due as the perspectives of future selves. Sometimes when we ask ourselves what we could possibly have been thinking back then, we really don't know. Nor do we really know what we *should* have been thinking. What we think we should have been thinking may have been impossible for us to think. Time brings greater knowledge, but it also takes knowledge away.

Moreover, knowing how our lives have turned out does not bring us any knowledge of how the alternatives would have turned out, even what seem the safest of paths. Determinations of risk and safety are relative determinations—relative to what matters to us. What in retrospect looks like a safe path might have turned out to be a very risky one. At the end of that path the self looking back might have decided that something that deeply matters had been lost. Without taking that path, we cannot know what that something is or whether it would have been lost.

That is what makes our most difficult decisions so difficult. We feel that either way we choose, regret cannot be ruled out. If Rawls tells me that the feeling can be dispelled with more reflection, all I can say back is that I don't know what else to reflect on. There comes a time in some deliberations when even the most important decisions of our lives seem as arbitrary as the choice in a restaurant between the blue crabs and the striped bass, and we can't be sure that we won't wish that we'd ordered the other.

Certainly, I would rather look back without regret, and just as certainly I hope that I do, but I don't feel at all assured that I will. My earlier choices have not been fully played out and too many important choices lie ahead. Whether the conviction that I'm doing the best I can will stave off regret if my best isn't good enough, or whether I will feel that I didn't do the best I can, I cannot know.

Nor do I know whether I should even concern myself with that. If the perspective of deliberation really is from here, perhaps what I need is something different from a rational life *plan*. I know what is important to me now and I order my life accordingly. Not too long ago other things were more important and my life was ordered differently. Perhaps the time will come when I regret the changes and I'll be able to go back, or do something different. Perhaps it will be too late. Perhaps that will matter to me, perhaps it won't. That is, perhaps the regret will not be a deep one. In such circumstances, the rational thing seems to be not to worry about it—to order my life around what's important to me now rather than what might be important to me later.

None of this is to say that our future selves are irrelevant to today's decisions. Some things that matter to us now matter only because we expect them to matter later. And to do something we *know* we'll deeply regret for the rest of our lives no doubt is irrational. But to do something we know we *might* deeply regret for the rest of our lives may be as good a description of the human condition as we're likely to get.

IF THAT LAST SENTENCE IS RIGHT, then Aristotle is wrong. There is no formula for eudaimonia. Morality is not, as Faulkner's Thomas Sutpen thought, like baking a cake.

On the other hand, perhaps it isn't Aristotle who went wrong, but the world. That's the view of Alisdair MacIntyre.[3] Sutpen's life plan foundered, MacIntyre would say, because it was a modern life plan in the modern world. That is the lesson of *Absalom, Absalom!*

But even more important, MacIntyre *did* say something like this: Nietzsche's challenge has the force it does only in the modern world, where Aristotle's conception of morality has been lost. Against an Aristotelian view, it is impotent. Thus, he ends *After Virtue* with his answer to a question posed earlier in the book. The question: Nietzsche or Aristotle? The answer: Aristotle. So let's turn to what MacIntyre has to say.

The first thing to note about it is that it is much more ambitious than what Rawls has to say about rational life plans. Rawls's ambition extends only to the powers of practical wisdom. He does not seek to answer Nietzsche's challenge with his rational life plan. An individual can live her good life without accepting society's conception of the good and its rules. MacIntyre's view of the good life *is* a response to Nietzsche's challenge.

MacIntyre's response can best be described as an attempt to restore unity to our moral lives, a unity that has been lost because of the modern, non-Aristotelian insistence on putting moral rules at the center of ethics. In doing so, the modern world has wrenched moral terms from the context that gives them meaning. We are,

MacIntyre says, like people in a post-scientific world who come across fragments of scientific discourse, put them together as best they can, and proceed to do "science." We have many of the right words, but our activity is in profound disorder. In a very real sense, we don't know what we're talking about. And because of that, we don't know how to live.

To understand the good life correctly, we require a certain kind of context. One thing we require is a moral community—not merely one that agrees on certain moral rules, but one that sees itself as engaging in shared practices. Practices, MacIntyre says, are complex social activities that require cooperation among the individuals who engage in them. They are marked by internal goods. To participate in them is to strive for standards of excellence that are both appropriate to them and definitive of them. Thus, they are also marked by their capacity to extend our ability to achieve a shared conception of both human excellence and the human good.

Of course, every society has such practices. Ours has physics and basketball, to name but two. But there is much that we don't have. For one thing, we don't have a shared sense of many of our most important activities as practices—citizenship, for example, or friendship, or, in many cases, family life. For another, we don't have a shared conception of how these practices are to be ordered in human lives. We have a shared conception of the right—the rules we are to follow—but our social and political community aims only to provide a climate in which each individual is free to define and pursue her own good. It seeks to provide certain goods, but not to define and achieve *the* human good.

That failure is closely related to another. We do not have a conception of the telos of a human life. We do not see our lives as narratives, stretching backward and forward in time, giving the episodes of our lives meaning. Thus, we have no sense of an appropriate narrative form—the search for the human good—or of an appropriate narrative setting—the community in which we find ourselves, our places and roles in it, the institutions and practices that, as much as our own decisions, give our lives narrative meaning and define the good for us. And, equally important, we lack the understanding of our narratives as part of a narrative tradition— a moral tradition that is *our* tradition, the one that provides *our* past and whose future *we* provide.

It is because we lack all of this that our lives lack moral unity. We can follow all of society's rules but still fail to live good lives because the rules cannot tell us how to live. And it is because the classical world did not lack these things that human lives in that world did not lack moral unity.

Moreover, there is one other thing that the classical world had that we do not—a virtue-based ethics, which is itself an expression of that moral unity. The virtues are the dispositions that enable us to attain the goods internal to our practices and our quest for the good. In acquiring and manifesting them, we both live good lives and fulfill social expectations of us. Key to virtue-centered ethics is this: Our good is found in our social roles and relations.

MUCH CAN BE SAID about MacIntyre's account. Most important for our purposes, it is difficult, probably impossible, to distinguish a personal and impersonal moral point of view in it. The moral life really is of a unity here. My personal conception of the good cannot be weighed against society's rules because both have been replaced. In MacIntyre's moral universe, I act honestly not because of society's rules or my personal moral code but because honesty is an excellence internally related to our practices. It is a good that is partly definitive of the good life. Thus, Nietzsche's challenge cannot arise.

Nor, for that matter, can Williams's, as MacIntyre's review of *Moral Luck* makes clear.[4] Williams, as he sees it, pits two incommensurable points of view against each other—the view of impersonal morality and the view from our own ground projects. By looking at our moral lives that way, he precludes any hope for a moral resolution. Suppose, though, that we were to think instead of one point of view—practices, with their own excellences and their own places in social life. Then the dilemmas mulled over by Williams would take on a different cast. Consider Gauguin's. Here we have a case of a man engaged in two practices, family life and art. Each has its own internal goods, but each also exists as part of a larger community alongside other practices, with their internal goods. Gauguin, of course, was a member of such a community and engaged in many of its practices. So a variety of virtues come into play, and the problem is not to decide between the demands of two radically different points of view, but to order the requirements of one. Conflict there may be, but not incommensurability.

Does that help Gauguin make his decision? Probably not, but that is because we live in the modern world, where each of us pursues his own good however he sees it, where each of us decides how his life is to be ordered. With no shared conception of the unified life, there is no way to make such a decision from the perspective of the full moral life. Presumably, we must first adopt the perspective of the full moral life and then work out the proper ordering.

Thus, MacIntyre's solution to our two challenges is not an immediate one. Before we can merge our conceptions of the good life and the good person, we must return to an Aristotelian world. And that is the second important thing to be said about it.

HERE'S THE THIRD: It is, in many respects, similar to the hopes Williams expresses in *Ethics and the Limits of Philosophy*. He, too, thinks we have more to learn from Aristotle than from Kant and his successors, just as he believes that the promise of a unified moral life lies in a moral outlook that emphasizes dispositions rather than rules. He also expresses his hope for a morality that offers us meaningful lives that share society's perceptions in considerable depth, which seems a fair characterization of MacIntyre's project.

Indeed, even Nietzsche, at least on one interpretation, would find some things to like. He did see himself, as MacIntyre notes, as an upholder of the classical tradition, however quirkily he interpreted it. Although he had few kind words for *virtue* (singular), he professed much respect for various *virtues* (plural). And it goes without saying that he felt that the question of how we are to live our lives must be answered in terms of the good life rather than moral rules, and that the good life involves the cultivation of the virtues he respected.

One thing, however, does not go without saying. Although MacIntyre (with some textual justification) portrays Nietzsche's ideal as a solitary, disconnected figure untied to tradition, that portrayal is not totally accurate.[5] What makes Zarathustra, say, so solitary is historical circumstance (plus Nietzsche's penchant for literary effect). Only *he* saw morality as mystification. He saw it as manmade, others as given by God or pure reason. He recognized it as historically conditioned and changeable, others as absolute. He celebrated heroic virtues, others the virtues required by the moral rules of the day. But he did envision a community of like-minded individuals, and he did recognize that the moral tradition could not be overturned all at once. His transvaluation of value, let's not forget, was to be a gradual process. (Let's not forget something else. MacIntyre counts rebellion as one way of recognizing one's tradition.)

Of course, we shouldn't downplay Nietzsche's radical individualism. He would not allow *his* good to be found in his social roles, nor would he let *his* virtues be dictated by the practices he engaged in. (Notice how many of the excellences internal to philosophy he ignored, which no doubt explains much of his appeal outside philosophy.) Nor would he have any truck with a moral universe in which his challenge could not arise. There, too, he would find mystification.

In much milder terms, we could say the same of Williams, who is also more of an individualist than MacIntyre. When he expressed his hope for a morality that offers meaningful life that shares society's perceptions in considerable depth, he did not stop there, but added this: It had to be a life enough unlike other lives, "in its opacities and disorders as well as in its reasoned intentions, to make it *somebody's*."[6] And he opposed that requirement to social planning and communal ritual. MacIntyre, on the other hand, has no affection for liberal individualism. He chides Marxism for being too individualistic and places his own hope in a new St. Benedict, who will provide the sort of social order required by his moral views.[7]

If MacIntyre does answer our two challenges, then, his answer is not acceptable to our challengers themselves.

BUT DOES HE? Whether he does depends on a variety of factors. One is whether his analogy to a post-scientific world is a good one, and if it is whether anything can be made of it. Certainly, morality

has changed, and with it ethics as a philosophical pursuit. But so
has science, and with it philosophy of science. It has, for example,
become increasingly difficult to talk of science and the scientific
method (both singular) as opposed to sciences and their methods
(both plural). And just as certainly, with the changes in ethics have
come many philosophical mistakes, which Nietzsche, among others,
was very adept at pointing out. (Parallel remarks can be made about
philosophy of science, of course.) But none of that shows that
morality is in a state of great conceptual disorder, nor does it show
that the classical tradition was free of any great conceptual disorder.
Indeed, that Aristotle's ethics rested on his highly suspect metaphysics suggests that we might have come a long way since.

To be sure, MacIntyre manages to free Aristotelian ethics from
Aristotelian metaphysics, but at high cost. Its role is taken by a
highly illiberal political and social structure. Whether it is possible
to return to such a structure is doubtful at best. Whether it is
desirable to do it is even more doubtful. To my mind, at least, there
is something unpleasantly Orwellian about a moral universe in
which neither of our challenges can even arise. MacIntyre's conceptually well-ordered moral discourse has something of the ring
of newspeak, in which the Declaration of Independence could not
be written. It leaves us a similar loss.

That loss is not one imposed on us by Rawls, who carefully
separates the good life from the good person.[8] Goodness is rationality, he tells us, and the life that is most rational for me to choose
need not be a life lived by the sort of person that people in a well-
ordered society could rationally desire to have among them. That
is, I can live my good life without being a morally good person.
Hence the possibility of our two challenges.

Nor is it a loss imposed on us by externalists like Baier. They
may read ideals and values out of *the* moral point of view, and they

may hold a view of practical reason that keeps them from realizing the full force of the challenges, but they certainly leave conceptual room for the conflicts that give rise to them. Moreover, at least one of them—Thomas Nagel—does recognize the full force of Williams's challenge, and his aptly titled *The View from Nowhere* devotes an entire chapter to it.[9]

Like Williams (and no doubt MacIntyre) Nagel finds the grounds for conflict between what he calls the good life and the moral life disturbing. Unlike Williams, he is unwilling to give up the hegemony of the impersonal point of view. The problem, as he sees it, is to decide from the impersonal point of view what allowances we can make for individual motivation and needs, to make impersonal morality's demands on individuals as reasonable as possible from the personal point of view in order to reduce the grounds for conflict as much as possible.

That is not only a fair *prescription* for us but a good *description* of how morality evolves. The social contract changes when the rules become increasingly unacceptable to individuals from the personal point of view. As women found it increasingly difficult to live good lives and accept the obligations that kept them bound to the home, we decided together to relax those obligations. And that was more than just a sensible thing to do. It was also, on neo-Kantian grounds, a good thing to do. If we want our rules to respect individual autonomy, we must want them to remove the grounds for conflict between the good life and obligation as much as possible.

But as Nagel well knows, the conflict cannot be totally eliminated by adjustments from the impersonal point of view. Thus, Williams's challenge ultimately becomes a political problem. We must create political institutions that minimize the grounds for conflict, and we must develop in our people the kinds of dispositions that enable them to live their good lives within the bounds of moral rules. Moral harmony, no less than civil peace, is a political task.

That, too, is both a fair prescription and a good description— as long as it is interpreted rightly. Nagel makes clear that he is not calling for the creation of a "new man" unlike ourselves. He also makes clear that he is not calling for a conflation of the two perspectives. The moral and political task is to create a context in which the demands of the impersonal perspective can be met while individuals remain free to pursue ideals and values that cannot, as he puts it, be impersonally acknowledged.

NAGEL'S WAY OF DEALING with Williams's challenge is, of course, firmly entrenched in the liberal tradition, and that is what makes it so much more appealing than MacIntyre's, which explicitly rejects that tradition. Instead of devising a framework in which the challenge does not arise, he does his best to accommodate the personal point of view from within the impersonal one. But for precisely that reason it is not an answer. Grounds for conflict will remain, and nothing Nagel says establishes the hegemony of the impersonal point of view in the lives of individuals.

MacIntyre rightly sees that outcome as inevitable. But he wrongly (at least to us inveterate liberals) thinks that his response is more appealing. Taking his cue from a passage by Nietzsche that describes the great man as isolated and self-absorbed, he compares the good life available in the modern world of liberal individualism with the good life promised by his own Aristotelian scheme.[10] The former he finds wanting, as most of us would. But Nietzsche's passage does not reflect the good lives that most of us pursue, and to say that Nietzsche's challenge cannot be met within our current moral framework is not to give any one of his passages any authority in the matter. To the contrary, the stronger Nietzsche's challenge, the more moral freedom we have to pursue our good lives as we see them. The appeal of both Nietzsche and Williams lies in their recognition that what most *matters* to us cannot be read out of our moral lives. And the appeal of Nagel lies in his attempt to accommodate that.

By the same token, MacIntyre's lack of appeal lies in his attempt to burke the issue. Let's return to his review of *Moral Luck*, where he raises an interesting criticism against Williams— that he has fallen victim to the magic of the pronoun *my*. The charge arises out of the following example. A man saves his wife's life rather than the life of someone who, objectively speaking, might be more worthy of being saved. To ask for justification of that, Williams says, is to ask for one thought too many. An individual's deep attachments to others must express themselves, apart from the demands of impersonal morality.[11]

MacIntyre agrees that to ask for justification may be to ask for one thought too many, not because it is *my* wife, but because it is my *wife*. And the deep attachment that makes further justification unnecessary, he says, is social, not psychological. Family life is a practice, having its own internal goods, its own virtues. The reason that Williams sees a conflict between deep attachment and the impersonal system is because he sees that system as being a matter of rules instead of practices.

If we don't take it too far, the point seems well taken. It is, after all, because she is my *wife* that only the strictest of act utilitarians would question the decision or ask for further justification. But that shows only that Williams's basic point is somewhat obscured by the example. There are many practices, many internal goods, many virtues, and they are not all of a piece. Not only are some of greater social importance, but many are of greater psychological importance, and that is a matter of great variation from individual to individual. Different things matter more deeply to some individuals than to others, and whether we see morality as rule-centered or virtue-centered, what matters most deeply to us can always raise grounds for conflict. Williams really meant *psychological* attachments. And from the personal point of view, they must remain of great importance. They define *my* good life, and to say that is not to have fallen victim to any magic. (The word "good" is every bit as important as "my.") It is, though, to say that our two challenges can still arise in MacIntyre's framework. My good life can still conflict with the demands of the impersonal system, and if that turns out to be somewhat incoherent according to MacIntyre's way of looking at things, so much the worse for his way of looking at things.

WE ARE LEFT, THEN, with the banalities about good lives. But one question remains. Are some good lives better than others?

Even if we confine ourselves to the banalities, the answer has to be yes. Otherwise, a good life would have to be a perfect life, and that would be to demand too much. A good life must allow for minor mistakes, minor failures, and minor regrets. Indeed, it must even allow, in some cases, for the kind of deep regret that leads an individual at the end of life to consider that life a failure. That was the point of adding the *ceteris paribus* condition to what I called Rawls's Second Aristotelian Principle.

Given two possible lives of the same person, both identical except that one ends in regret, certainly the one that does not is a better one. But to say that a life that ends in deep regret is therefore not a good one is to give too little weight to the judgments the individual made while living most of it. It is also to make the final judgment incorrigible—to make the temporally final word the authoritatively final word. And it is to make the most irrelevant contingencies—that somebody is hit by a truck on her way into a restaurant rather than on her way back to her car, say—the decisive factor in whether someone has led a good life.

Moreover, some good lives are morally better than others from the impersonal point of view. That, of course, is a consequence of our continuing failure to meet our two challenges. Someone can live her good life without, from the impersonal point of view, living a morally good one.

In raising these points, I raise nothing new. They follow straight-forwardly from what has preceded them. The next point does not. It arises from the principle that Rawls calls his Aristotelian Principle (what I called his First Aristotelian Principle), to which we now turn.

RAWLS'S ARISTOTELIAN PRINCIPLE is a psychological principle. Other things being equal, we enjoy exercising our realized capacities. The more the capacity is realized, the greater the enjoyment. The more complex the capacity, the greater the enjoyment. Thus, we are generally motivated to develop our capacities and to exercise our most complex capacities. A skilled auto mechanic prefers working at his trade to performing a simple repetitive task on an assembly line. A chess player who knows how to play checkers prefers chess. A music lover who understands both classical and popular music prefers listening to classical.

The *ceteris paribus* condition is important here. All kinds of considerations can affect our choices. Since I don't like Wagner, I prefer listening to a good recording of a Rodgers and Hart tune. I do like Mozart, but *Don Giovanni* makes poor background music during the cocktail hour. And very often I'm just too tired to read Chekhov instead of watching a "Barney Miller" rerun.

More generally, the *ceteris paribus* condition allows for a good deal of individual difference. Variation in talents, skills and interests will make a big difference in which capacities we choose to develop and how far we choose to develop them. The faint-hearted are unlikely to take up downhill skiing, the aesthetically blind to make too many disappointing trips to art museums, and the clumsy to continue bashing their thumbs with hammers to better their home-improvement skills.

Moreover, depending on a variety of factors—the strenuousness of their daily routines, say—individuals will be more or less inclined to put much effort into greater development of even their favorite capacities. Each individual must balance anticipated rewards of greater development against the difficulties, inconveniences, and other disadvantages of greater development. Rawls imagines as a limiting case a man whose only interest is counting blades of grass. If we assume that his own balancing calculations are correct, that developing and exercising other capacities really aren't worth the effort to him, we cannot fault his choice. The Aristotelian Principle is, again, merely a principle about human motivation.

For Aristotle himself, of course, it was much more. It was a principle of value. A life in which certain capacities are not developed cannot be as good as one in which they are. Most important, *the* good life requires the development and exercise of the intellect. Mill, with his famous comparison of the satisfied pig and dissatisfied philosopher, agreed.

So does Hilary Putnam, who asks us to imagine a society of "pig-men," farmers with a total lack of interest in cultural or spiritual life or, for that matter, anything that doesn't relate directly to their farming.[12] Is there not, he asks, something contemptible about their lives?

Most of us would say yes. But we would also assume, as Putnam does, that they are capable of living richer and more varied lives and, given the appropriate knowledge and opportunity, would prefer to live such lives. But what if they are ideologically fanatical pig-men? What if their reasoned judgment is that their pig-lives are the best lives? What if their lives are the result of choice rather than lack of opportunity? Can we then say that our lives are better than theirs? Not just better for us, but better, period.

IT IS HARD TO IMAGINE such a society. But it is not hard to imagine people with no interest in science, philosophy, art, or literature. In fact, we don't have to imagine them. They are among the ordinary mortals I mentioned in the third chapter, the beer-drinking, pop-corn-munching television watchers with no interest in the life of the mind. If we assume that they are content with their lives, that they judge their lives good ones, if we assume that they really have no reason to change their ways, that they will judge their lives worse if they do, is it mere snobbery to say that their lives would have been better if they had been able to live different ones?

To ask that question is to pose what might be called the ordinary mortal's challenge to Aristotle. It is to pose the challenge implicit in the question asked by many undergraduates: Why should they study philosophy or literature or anything else of no practical use (ouch!)? When my students ask me that, I refer them to a recurring line from the film *Two for the Road*, which is something like this: What kind of people sit at a table without even trying to talk to each other? Married people.

That is not just a witty line, I tell them. It captures a surprising number of couples I come across in central Wisconsin restaurants— young, middle-aged, and old couples who don't even look at each other, let alone try to converse. When groups of married couples go out, they are usually quite boisterous, but when one couple goes out, husband and wife stare stonily past each other.

I often wonder what they're thinking as they sit in silence, my answer continues. Do they wish they had something to say to each other? Do they have something to say but decide not to say it because they already know the response? Are they deliberately avoiding each other's eyes, or are they barely aware of each other? Are they daydreaming? Do they wish that other couples were with them? Or are their minds as blank as their stares? I wonder also about their lives at home—whether they talk to each other only when necessary, whether they're bored with each other, happy with each other, whether they genuinely like each other.

The lives that I imagine seem incredibly barren. But what do I know of them? We are, after all, products of different cultures. But their culture is the same as many of my students', and I do know this: When I tell my students about the possibility of richer lives and the role that a liberal education can play in making that possibility real, they take my words as a reasonable answer to their question. They believe me when I tell them that to be familiar with the stories of Chekhov, the music of Mozart, the images of Vermeer, is to be regularly reminded of them—just as I am reminded of the line from *Two for the Road* whenever I go out to dinner—and that to be reminded of them is to bring something extra to every experience, to have a variety of ways of absorbing and responding to it. And they agree with me when I tell them that it is also to get more out of life—and that it is the way that many husbands and wives remain interesting to each other.

Good Lives

THAT THEY DO BELIEVE and agree with me suggests that an Aristotelian view about ranking of good lives cannot be *merely* snobbery. Indeed, it is difficult to imagine anybody denying that, other things being equal, a richer life is a better life. That is why it is so hard to imagine ideologically fanatical pig-men, or Rawls's grass counter.

But the examples I give them are selected from a very narrow range, the range I am asked to justify. Can the same things be said about athletics, tinkering with cars, cooking, doing challenging puzzles, and other complex activities that I am not asked to justify? Can they also be said about popular culture? The temptation is to say no. The way I present my examples suggests that they offer a richness of a different order, a richness that is not self-contained but is capable of transforming the rest of our lives in a way that the others cannot.

But that may be a prejudice. *Two for the Road*, after all, is a piece of popular culture, and it is the reverberations from it, not Chekhov, that spark my answer. We should not confuse the relative artistic and intellectual merits of popular culture and the culture we offer in a liberal curriculum with the roles that each is capable of playing in the particular lives of particular individuals. Nor should we forget the many ways that a house or piece of furniture can present itself to a carpenter but can't present itself to someone who sees a hammer as a threat to his thumb, or the richness that can come from what—to at least this academic—seem to be incomprehensible tribal rituals, like deer-hunting season in Wisconsin.

To most of my students, debates about the relative merits of the tabula rasa and veined marble metaphors are equally incomprehensible tribal rituals. That is why even many who accept my answer eventually decide to take their three humanities credits and run. If they have missed an opportunity to add richness to their lives, they have not missed the only one.

But what about the silent couples? If their lives are indeed barren, then of course they are not as good as they could be. But engaging in the world of culture is not the only antidote for barrenness, nor is it a sure one. And if their lives are not barren, the problem—if it is one—may be relatively small to them, as small as many imperfections in the lives of those of us who do enjoy talking to our spouses at dinner.

ONCE AGAIN, THEN, we are left with the banalities about the good life. The more meaningful we judge our lives, the better our lives. The greater our sense of self-worth, the better our lives. The wiser we take our choices to be, the better our lives. The less our desires are frustrated, the better our lives. And the richer our lives, the better our lives.

And, once again, we are left with our two challenges unmet. But we have found the basis for a new way of distinguishing them. In discussing Rawls, I mentioned (and passed over) his account of a morally good person—someone who has the broadly based character traits that it is rational for the members of a well-ordered society to want in the people who live among them. Those broadly based character traits are what he calls the moral virtues. If we take his account to be at least roughly adequate, we can say the following. Nietzsche's challenge, the stronger of the two, asks why we should adopt the "moral" virtues as our virtues. It asks why living *my* good life cannot take moral precedence over being a "good" person. Williams's challenge, the weaker one, does not ask the first question. Although he realizes, with Nietzsche, that it can be perfectly rational to reject the moral virtues, he also takes it as a given that the moral life requires that we not reject them. His challenge concerns the role of these virtues in our full moral lives. (He, of course, would say "ethical lives.")

Let's put the matter somewhat differently. Let's talk of decent people instead of morally good people, and let's think of a decent person as someone who is generally disposed to act fairly and kindly toward others. A decent person will not poison his lover and photograph her death throes, but he might quit an unsatisfying job to begin a new life as a free-lancer, even though he knows that his decision will mean some financial hardship for his family. A decent person is not a selfish one. He knows that others have legitimate demands on him and he is generally disposed to meet them. But he may feel in some cases that he cannot afford to meet them—that they require him to sacrifice too much of his own good. Normal demands may, for him, become supererogatory. And that is the heart of Williams's challenge.

The heart of Nietzsche's challenge is more disturbing, because it may lead to a challenge to decency itself. As both a moralist and an anti-moralist, he challenges us to recognize that a personal moral code that no decent person could adopt may be no less moral for it. (That is not to say that Nietzsche himself championed such a morality. Whether he did is a matter of endless debate, which I'll let others pretend to settle.) He challenges us to recognize that some normal demands may be irrelevant to the moral lives of some people—that a moral person might not be a decent one.

Impersonal morality can, as Nagel says, bend a bit to accommodate Williams's challenge. It cannot bend enough to meet Nietzsche's. It can widen the range of the supererogatory, but it cannot accept a lack of decency. It can accept many good lives that give Rawls's moral virtues less weight than morally better lives from its own point of view, but it cannot accept good lives that reject them. If there is a best impersonal morality, a best set of moral rules, it is a morality that, among other things, allows as many people as possible to live their good lives in ways that can be accepted. And that is the topic of the next chapter.

6

BETTER MORALITIES

WHAT MAKES SOME MORALITIES better than others? I have given a variety of answers to that question. The more it accords with common sense, the better the morality. The fewer the invalid rules, the better the morality. The more freely chosen the rules, the better the morality. The better it advances a shared conception of the good, the better the morality. The more moral freedom it gives individuals to pursue their own good lives, the better the morality. And the more easily it can be incorporated into the personal moral lives of individuals, the better the morality.

In this chapter, I will be primarily concerned with the last two answers. They are, I think, closely related—at least for those of us with a liberal bent. What we want, following Williams, is a morality that allows individuals to share society's perceptions yet live good lives that are felt to be distinctively their own. Such a morality would be one that makes significant concessions to the personal point of view. It would recognize that an individual's considered judgment that such and such is the best thing for *him* to do has considerable moral weight against the judgment that *one ought* to do something else. It would, following Nagel, widen the range of the supererogatory and recognize that, in a variety of cases, requiring

Better Moralities

a particular individual to do what one ought to do is to require too much.

One way of achieving that end is to allow individuals to weigh their obligations from the personal point of view—that is, to incorporate the impersonal point of view into the personal. Of course, as I noted in the previous chapter, impersonal morality can bend only so far in that regard. It can, I think, bend far enough to accommodate Williams's challenge, but not Nietzsche's.

In what follows, I give my view of how that end can best be achieved. I begin with some—admittedly impressionistic—reflections on how many ordinary people do incorporate impersonal morality into their moral lives.

IT'S A POINT OFTEN MENTIONED and often neglected. Impersonal morality—determining what one ought to do from the impersonal point of view—doesn't matter much to many people. We don't much like to hurt others so most of us don't do much that is wrong, but we don't often avoid doing wrong because one ought not do it.

Philippa Foot made the point—or, more properly, a related point—quite forcefully in her well known assault on the idea of a categorical imperative.[1] Not only is there no such thing as a categorical imperative, she wrote, but it doesn't matter that there isn't. We act more or less decently because we want to be more or less decent people, so hypothetical imperatives will do quite nicely.

Of course, Foot's observation is not the same as mine. People might care deeply about doing what one ought to do because of their concern for others, and so they might often do the right thing because one ought to do it. Perhaps some people are like that. But not many, it seems.

Again, we don't like to hurt people so we avoid hurting people and thereby avoid doing many wrong things. But if nobody's going to be hurt in any direct or obvious way, many of us are much less likely to avoid doing the wrong thing. Most people—most people I know, at least—have no trouble lying for their friends. If one friend asks another to tell his wife he was with him last night, he will. It is easy enough to say that we don't think lying wrong in such cases, but I have serious doubts about that. Assuming that all of us have some allegiance to the golden rule, and assuming that most of us—if not all of us—would *not* want to be lied to in such cases, how can we plausibly maintain that we don't think it wrong from the impersonal point of view? Granted, we are doing for the friend as we might want him to do for us, but we are not doing to the wife as we would want her to do to us.

Of course, in other cases we can plausibly maintain that lying for a friend *is* morally acceptable from the impersonal point of view. I'd rather be told that Jane's not home than be told that she has no desire to talk to me, so I see nothing wrong with telling that kind of lie. But I certainly would not want to be lied to about my wife's infidelity. Yet I'd tell such a lie anyway. Of course, if my sympathies are more with the wife than the husband, I'd probably not tell the lie. But that does not mean that I'm now concerned with right and wrong. Whether my sympathies are more with the husband or the wife, my concern is not with what one ought to do. In either case, what things boil down to is this: I want to be nice to my friends.

THE PURPOSE OF THE ABOVE is to make a point that underlies much of this book. Most of us are more concerned with what kind of people we want to be than with what impersonal morality demands that we do. Most of us are more concerned, therefore, with what the best thing for us to do is than with what one ought to do. And we don't think ourselves immoral for that. We are spared Dostoevskian consciences—not because a conscience is inconvenient, but because we consider the people we want to be good people.

Some philosophers have, to varying degrees, come to believe that there is something right about all of this. They believe not only that things *are* this way for most people, but that it's *good* that they are, that doing the right thing is one value among many values and that a world in which other values—even Paul Newman's cool and Groucho Marx's sarcastic wit, as Susan Wolf would have it—are allowed to flourish at its expense is a desirable world.[2] Other moral philosophers—more, apparently—disagree. The demands of impersonal morality are and must be overriding. And if some other value like friendship conflicts with these demands, then, as Marcia Baron has put it, so much the worse for friendship.[3]

Setting aside externalist arguments for this conclusion, we might ask *why*? What makes impersonal moral values predominant? Why have moral philosophers stressed moral duty so strongly?

Nietzsche had an answer to that question: Fear. Morality is concerned with safety, and rule-followers are safe. Although Kant would no doubt have denied having any such motivation, neo-Kantians and social contract theorists seem implicitly to concede it. The dangers of people acting according to their own self-interest, the dangers of a lapse into the state of nature, seem always to be lurking.

Whether fear really is a motivating factor here is not for me to say, but one thing seems clear. We have little to fear from nice people, even immoral nice people. The Jack Lemmon character in Billy Wilder's film *The Apartment* is certainly a nice man—he means no harm to others—and he is just as certainly a safe one, regardless of the immorality of climbing the corporate ladder by giving out one's apartment keys to philandering executives.

What's wrong with nice immoral people, then, if we have little to fear from them? One thing is this: They can't always be trusted. A nice but not particularly moral person will not keep agreements if they get in the way of doing the nice thing. Nor will he let fairness or honesty get in the way of doing the nice thing. He may give special favors to his friends, for instance, look the other way when they cheat, break a promise because he "didn't have the heart" to do whatever he promised to do. He will not deliberately hurt us, but he will not concern himself with the social contract either. With enough such people, we might wonder, won't the social contract break down?

Perhaps, but more likely it will just change, become more relaxed. Perhaps it already is more relaxed than some moral philosophers think.

I have already noted that many of us break promises out of mere convenience and allow that others will do the same, and that we don't complain when others do it and don't expect others to complain when we do. I might add now that we often take "I didn't have the heart" as a legitimate justification for the breaking of various promises. Niceness justifies—or at least excuses— much, and we are too nice not to recognize that—as long as nobody is seriously hurt by the broken promise. As they often say in basketball circles: no harm, no foul.

Of course, we have to keep closer tabs on people who are nice but not particularly moral. Nice but not particularly moral students, for example, will be more likely to cheat or allow others to cheat (and we, also being nice, will usually deal more harshly with the student who turned in another's paper as his own than with the student who lent the paper). And the nice but not particularly moral person like Jack Lemmon's "Buddy Boy," as the borrowers of his keys called him, might get the promotion that we deserve. But all in all, laxity doesn't spell disaster.

The biggest problem with the nice but not particularly moral person is that he has no *character*. He's *unprincipled*. Buddy Boy is nice enough, but he is also a *schlemiel*, a nebbish, a *schlepper*, someone decidedly not to be admired. But being unprincipled and not concerning oneself with moral rules are not the same thing. G. Gordon Liddy is hardly an unprincipled man, and he certainly displayed a good deal of character during the Watergate affair. He may not have followed society's rules, but he was true to his own moral code: He served his prince.

What the Liddy example shows is that we can have much more to fear from a principled man than an unprincipled one. Strength of character may be an admirable trait, but we are safer with unprincipled people as long as they're nice.

That's why we prefer our principled people to be nice, too, or to be concerned with doing the right thing. Does it matter which?

TO ASK THAT QUESTION is to ask how important moral rules are. The standard answer, of course, is that they are of crucial importance. As I said in the first chapter, society without cooperation is impossible, and cooperation without moral rules is impossible.

I said that, and I'm not going to take it back, but I do want to take a skeptical look at it. Certainly, society without moral rules is not logically impossible, as society without cooperation seems plausibly to be. If people were strongly disposed to do what they said they were going to do, we would need no such institution as promising. And if they were strongly disposed to say only what they believe to be true, we would need no rules about honesty. Cooperation requires predictability, and we predict behavior of others based on our knowledge of their dispositions.

But most people are at most weakly disposed to do something merely because they say they're going to do it. We do, after all, change our minds quite frequently. What promising adds is a reason not to change our minds: I said I'll do it, you're counting on me to do it, if I don't do it you'll suffer some harm, so I'll do it, even though if it weren't for the promise I wouldn't.

One way of putting the point is to say that promising has created an obligation. Another is to say that a rule now applies. Put still another way, we have a new disposition to be encouraged—to do what we say we'll do if we have told someone they can count on us to do it.

So we do need such obligations, or rules. But it is important to be clear about who the *we* is here. It is we in a complex society. The more complex the society, the more intricate and extended the interactions, the more we are forced to rely on people doing what they tell us they will do, the more we need such rules. We could not have gotten where we are without them, and we cannot remain where we are without them.

Moreover, we must be clear about what we need them for—the development of the dispositions required for cooperation. Concern for others is a very general disposition. Doing what we say we'll do because we have given others reason to count on our doing it is a very specific one. There seems to be no difference between inculcating this specific disposition and teaching someone to fulfill a particular obligation or follow a particular rule.

Put another way, without knowing the rules we would not know how to be nice, just as we couldn't be good basketball players without knowing how the game is played. We could be talented enough (just as we could have our hearts in the right place) but we would not be an asset to any team that put us in the game (just as we would not be able to put our heads where our hearts are).

That makes moral rules important even for those of us who don't care much about doing the right thing but do care a lot about being nice. And that suggests something both interesting and important. It suggests a certain cleavage between being concerned about our obligations and being concerned about doing the right thing—or, to put the matter in a slightly different way, between caring about our prima facie duties and caring about our duties sans phrase. If I want to be a nice person, I have to know what my obligations to others, my prima facie duties, are. But I don't have to know what my actual duties are. I don't have to know what the right thing to do is. To worry about that is not to worry about being a nice person, but it is to worry about being—at least from the impersonal point of view—a moral person.

So let me rephrase the point I've been making. It is not correct to say that nice people don't care much about the demands of impersonal morality. What is correct is that they don't care much about doing the right thing. When prima facie duties conflict, they don't so much care about which takes precedence (their actual duty sans phrase) but about the one they would rather follow, the one *they* most care about. Their concern is to do the best thing for them to do, rather than do what one ought to do.

Or, put still another way, such people care most about what kind of people they are, and certain dispositions to fulfill various obligations are a large part of being what they want to be, but figuring out the right thing to do is not. Such people care more about who they are than what they do. They want to be good people, but not necessarily do what's right. They personalize the demands of impersonal morality, integrate them with their other values. And when they choose what to do, they choose from the personal point of view.

WILL SUCH PEOPLE do the wrong thing more often than we'd like? Certainly, they'll do the wrong thing more often than someone whose guiding principle is always to do what one ought to do. But now that I've conceded the importance of prima facie duties, we have to ask whether doing the right thing is of equal importance, or even of considerable importance. The answer, I think, is that the right thing doesn't matter nearly as much as most philosophers seem to think.

Much of our—moral philosophers'—concern with the right thing is, after all, theoretical. We want to decide between utilitarian and deontological theories, for example. We note that Mill and Ross agree that, other things being equal, we ought not lie, cheat, steal, and so forth. Are such prohibitions utilitarian rules of thumb, we ask, or prima facie duties? Well, find instances where they conflict and then see whether a direct appeal to utility agrees with our intuitions.

Recently, to be sure, much of our concern has been more practical. We do business ethics and medical ethics and discuss abortion and capital punishment and the like and ask ourselves what course of action is right in various circumstances. And, although our intuitions usually agree in the standard test cases against act utilitarianism, on these practical matters our opinions often sharply disagree.

Perhaps we disagree because, as Derek Parfit would have it, atheistic ethics is a young science.[4] Perhaps we disagree because, as many people would have it, there is no fact of the matter. And perhaps we disagree because (and this is perfectly consistent with either of the first two possibilities) we are different people with different dispositions, and regardless of how much we may agree on moral principles, prima facie duties and obligations, we personalize morality in decidedly different ways. Different things matter to us, and the same things matter to us to different degrees, and when we get down to particular cases how much different things matter must make a real difference even when we try to discuss practical problems from the impersonal point of view.

That, I think, is how most ordinary people look at it, which is why—excepting ideologues (true believers of various religious and political persuasions)—most of them are rarely concerned with settling questions of right and wrong in particular cases or kinds of cases. And that holds not only for their own behavior, but for the behavior of others.

To be sure, they sometimes feel wronged. Sometimes they will say so to the people they feel have wronged them. But if they get a decent response ("I didn't have the heart to keep my promise," say) that is often the end of the matter. They may continue to feel wronged, but they are mollified because they now understand that there is another acceptable—although not necessarily compelling—way of looking at what happened. The important issue, then, is not whether Jack wronged Jane, but whether Jack's way of looking at things is acceptable to Jane. Do the values that mattered most to him present themselves to her as understandably mattering that much? Are they the sorts of values that a decent person, in her eyes, might give such importance to? For such people, personal values are not interlopers in *the* moral point of view, nor do they divert us from the task at hand—determining what one ought to do or should have done. Acceptable personal moralities mark out a wide range of acceptable behaviors where the impersonal point of view might mark out only one act as right, and for most people, it seems, morality is about the former.

Better Moralities

IF THIS BRIEF EXERCISE in moral phenomenology is close to the mark, modern society has come a long way to achieving what Williams envisioned at the end of *Ethics and the Limits of Philosophy*—a meaningful life that shares society's perceptions in depth but is enough itself to be somebody's. It has done so, in large part, by taking the emphasis off the *right* and placing it on *nice* or *decent* behavior, by making morality personal enough to allow individuals wide latitude to determine how much weight to give their obligations—against other obligations, against their own ground projects, and even, at times, against mere convenience. And, again excepting ideologues, most ordinary people would agree that disaster has not befallen us as a result.

Then again, even most *non*ideologues will agree that disaster is not the only undesirable outcome. Unseemliness is another, and an emphasis on niceness rather than rightness can and does produce a lot of that. Buddy Boy's behavior is unseemly. So, to many of us, is the behavior of students who help other students cheat. So, to some, is the behavior of those of us who are willing to cover up their friends' infidelities. Sleaziness is another undesirable outcome, and, like unseemliness, it too can and does result from a de-emphasis on rightness. Insider trading scandals are sleazy. So are various instances of former White House officials cashing in on their high-placed connections.

Why do unseemliness and sleaze result from a shift of emphasis from right to nice? Because nice people who are not particularly concerned to do the right thing are not likely to avoid doing wrong if no obvious or direct harm will come to others because of it. That's one answer I gave earlier. Another is this: Nice people like Buddy Boy have no character. They're unprincipled.

Fortunately, many nice people do have character. Many nice people are people of principle. Such people have some real commitment to strongly held values, the ability to distinguish the best thing for them to do from what's in their self interest, and the character to act on that. Some will not help a friend cheat—in a marriage, on a test, or in anything else—because they have an almost exceptionless commitment to honesty. Others may help in some cases but not in others—some, because marital values matter more to them than their desire to help their friends, some, because academic values matter more, and some, because some other internal goods matter more.

Such people are more likely to avoid doing wrong than people like Buddy Boy, and that's one reason we can count ourselves fortunate that many nice people are also principled people. But it's not the only reason, nor is it, for many people, the most important one. For those who are not often concerned with settling issues of right and wrong, for those who allow that morality has a strongly personal component, principled behavior, like nice behavior, is valued in and of itself. Principle, like niceness, justifies or excuses much. What matters is that the principles be acceptable ones, and that they be conjoined with niceness. Without niceness, a principled person can be cold and ruthless, like Liddy. Without principles, a nice person can be a *schlemiel*, like Buddy Boy.

IN THE PREVIOUS CHAPTER, I characterized a decent person as someone who cares about his obligations and is disposed to treat others kindly and fairly. In light of the foregoing, I can also characterize a decent person this way: someone who is both nice and acts on principles that others find acceptable.

And, also in light of the foregoing, we can say this: Given a society of decent people, debates about right and wrong from the impersonal point of view can seem like exercises in scholastic metaphysics—of concern only to the ideologues. To set out an array of related cases and ask of each one whether it is right to keep or break a promise, or whether it is right to tell the truth or dissemble, or whether it is right to report a wrongdoing or keep silent, or whether it is right to save John's life or Mary's life if we can't save both may have a certain theoretical interest, but can hardly be of practical interest to people who agree that a decent person might very well do either and that the proper decision is the one that some particular decent individual takes to be best.

Of course, they might be misguided. We might even say that the culprit is their moral education. Most of us do not learn morality as moral casuistry. What we learn instead is to adopt various moral virtues—kindness, honesty, generosity, respect, loyalty, and the like—as our own. Although nobody could seriously object to the inculcation of such dispositions, some people might say that the purpose of inculcating them is to get people to do the right thing. What ultimately matters is right behavior, not decency.

But as far as I can tell, that is a mere prejudice. I don't know whether Rawls shares it or not, but I find it interesting that his good people—those we would rationally welcome into our well-ordered society—are people with the right dispositions, not people who always do—or try to do—the right thing. I, at any rate, would prefer a society of decent people to moral saints. So, of course, would Susan Wolf.[5] But even more important, there is this point: Where decency is stressed over moral duty, individuals are granted greater moral freedom to pursue their own good lives.

My suggestion, then, is this: Let moral philosophy also shift its emphasis from the right to decency.

And the question that naturally follows is this: How?

Better Moralities

TO ANSWER THAT QUESTION, we must return to Nagel's suggestion for dealing with Williams's challenge. Actually, we needn't *return* to it at all, because much of the foregoing has been an examination of how ordinary morality has more or less taken it up. Nagel's suggestion, again, is that we widen the range of the supererogatory. And one way of putting the foregoing is to say that ordinary morality has widened it considerably. Ordinary morality requires no more of us than decency.

Although it is easy enough to say, "Let moral philosophy do the same," we must be careful about one important point. We must ask whether we want to require merely that people *be* decent people or whether, more strongly, we want to require that they *act* decently. Decent people may and often do, after all, have a variety of failings. They may be irresponsible, impetuous, rude, stingy, surly, lazy and any number of things. Moreover, the extent to which they care about the effects of their actions on others can vary. So can the obligations that matter to them and the weight they give them. So can the principles they adhere to and the strength with which they adhere to them. In short, otherwise decent people don't always act decently.

Williams's imagined Gauguin is a decent person, for instance, but in turning his back on his obligations to his family he does not act decently. The same can be said about many people who frequently break relatively trivial promises, or the habitually tardy who cause others to suffer minor or major inconveniences because of their tardiness. It can also be said about some students who occasionally cheat on exams—otherwise decent people who would never, say, cheat in a poker game or fail to return a found wallet. The decent Gauguin recognized his obligations to his family but forsook them for a meaningful life. The decent but irresponsible promise breakers care about their promises, but give short shrift to minor ones. The decent exam-cheaters value honesty when dishonesty causes obvious harm to others but care little about honesty when dishonesty does not. If we require only that people *be* decent, we say, in effect, that it would be supererogatory for the irresponsible to keep their promises and the exam cheaters to take their *F*'s. If we require that they *act* decently, we cannot say that it would have been supererogatory for Gauguin to have foregone his good life.

If, as I do, we think there is an important moral difference between Gauguin and the others, we must recognize that neither answer— requiring that people *be* decent or requiring that they *act* decently— will do. What we must do, then, is look for relevant differences.

Well, one thing about Williams's Gauguin is that his decision to leave his family comes after a good deal of soul-searching and reflection. He is a decent man whose best all-things-considered judgment is that the best thing for him to do is go off to paint. That cannot be said about the decent but irresponsible people who are lax when it comes to their smaller obligations. Most of us are willing to condone or excuse their lapses as minor peccadillos, but we are not willing to go so far as to say that their character flaws *justify* their behavior. The difference between them and Gauguin, then, is that their lapses are just that—lapses, not well-considered judgments about the best thing for them to do. Gauguin's behavior is justified, theirs merely explained.

The same may be said about some cheaters, but, more likely than not, matters are different. What they usually display is an indifference toward or contempt for a particular moral rule—don't cheat on exams. Or, we might say, they lack sufficient adherence to a particular principle—honesty. Or, we might also say, they lack a particular virtue—call it integrity, or honor. To be sure, the kind of person I have in mind is not thoroughly dishonest or dishonorable. He will not cheat in a poker game, nor will he make questionable calls in his own favor in a friendly game of tennis. He is, again, a decent person who has no desire to hurt others and cares about particular obligations to particular people and adheres to various other principles that the rest of us share, but victimless dishonesty counts for little or nothing to him. Unlike Williams's Gauguin, he is not an *honorable* decent person.

What we must do, then, is stress honor as well as decency. Also, we must recognize that, even though an honorable and decent person may not always act honorably or decently, fulfilling an obligation is supererogatory for him only if his all-things-considered judgment would be that the best thing for him to do is not to fulfill it.

THE IDEA BEHIND THAT LAST SUGGESTION is straightforward. All of us have obligations. To enter into social relations is to incur obligations. We also have personal values, commitments and ground projects. We also have concern for our own interests. When we deliberate over what the best thing for us to do is, we will, if we are decent and honorable people, take all into account. Our obligations and the effects of our decisions on others will, along with our self-interest and projects, matter to us.

When such a person deliberates carefully, she may choose to fulfill her obligations or, if they conflict, the ones that matter most to her. In either case, she acts decently. She may choose instead to pursue a deeply held good at the expense of her obligations. In that case, she may not act decently, but as long as her decision is the product of careful deliberation by an honorable and decent person, we should consider it morally acceptable. We should allow that it would be supererogatory for that person in that situation to choose otherwise.

To allow that is to reverse the view of neo-Kantian externalists, who, like Baier, claim that the rational thing to do is whatever is required from the impersonal point of view. Instead of saying that what is morally overriding from the impersonal point of view is rationally overriding for an individual, I am saying that what is rationally overriding from the personal point of view of a decent and honorable person is morally overriding for that person.

MANY PEOPLE WILL, OF COURSE, find fault with this reversal, independent of any externalist arguments. With some of the fault-finders, I am sympathetic. Those are the ones who will object to the looseness or fuzziness of it all. How honorable must a person be before we can count her as honorable enough? How decent must she be before we can count her as decent enough? How much weight must she characteristically give to the effects of her actions on others, to her obligations, to her principles?

Although I'm sympathetic, I'm afraid I don't have a ready answer. I don't know how many times, or on precisely what kinds of occasion, a person can act otherwise and still be considered a decent and honorable person. Most of us, however, seem to know one when we see one. What we seem to rely on when making the judgment are the attitudes the person does or doesn't express— most notably, indifference and contempt. Consider again the photographer who poisoned his lover to record on film her final, painful minutes. Not only did he display an utter indifference toward her life, her suffering, but he displayed an utterly incomprehensible indifference. How could a series of photographs matter more to him than *her*? Such a person is incomprehensibly contemptuous of anything we associate with decency, and no amount of otherwise decent behavior would convince us that he was a decent person.

The key word is *incomprehensible*. People might very well display comprehensible indifference or contempt toward others and still be counted decent people—a father who displays contempt for the life of his child's murderer, say, or a general who displays indifference toward the lives of enemy troops defending the beach his own troops must take.

On the other hand, people might display only comprehensible indifference or contempt yet still be counted indecent or dishonorable. What sets them apart is the existence of unacceptable patterns—habitual bullying, cheating or lying, for example, or any other pattern of indifference or contempt for obligations of honor or decency. The key word this time is "unacceptable." What makes such a pattern unacceptable is that we cannot excuse or condone its instances as mere lapses.

That, of course, may still leave the matter a bit too loose and fuzzy. The same may be said for (against?) the other part of the reversal. What is to count as a person's all-things-considered best judgment? The problem here is, in part, the same one encountered in my earlier discussion of Williams's account of reasons. Then I asked this question: Who knows how many reasons for staying with my wife I would discover upon careful reflection? I might now ask this one: Who knows how many reasons for keeping a particular obligation I would discover upon careful reflection? And the answer is: Not I. Nor do I know how careful the reflection must be before it is careful enough. That is the other part of the problem.

In short, whatever imprecision is inherent to practical rationality automatically attaches to morality. That seems to me unavoidable. So despite my sympathy with these anticipated fault-finders, I must repeat what I said in the third chapter. Artificial precision is no virtue.

WITH OTHER ANTICIPATED FAULT-FINDERS I am not sympathetic— those who will object to the built-in relativism of the reversal. That relativism appears in two places.

In the first, we have a form of individual relativism. Whether fulfilling an obligation is supererogatory for a particular individual is determined from the personal point of view. Although Nagel did not spell out how he would widen the range of the supererogatory, I doubt he would do it that way. Still, I think it the right way.

I don't have any arguments to support that thought, but I don't think that makes it a mere prejudice. The best I can say in my own defense is this: As long as Williams's challenge has not been met, I can think of no surer way to give a decent and honorable person's conception of the good its due.

In the second, we have a form of societal relativism. A decent and honorable person is characterized in terms of acceptable principles, patterns of behavior and the like. But acceptable to whom? To the society in which he lives. I don't know how widely such acceptability can vary from society to society, or, for that matter, how much it does vary. Nor do I know how widely the range of obligations can or does vary from society to society. Presumably, these variations depend on others—variations in social, political, and economic systems, and in shared ideals, valued activities, and the like.

That a morality that emphasizes the personal point of view over the impersonal one is better than one that does not, I have no doubt. That some social, political, and economic systems are better than others, I also have no doubt. Whether there is a best of each, and whether there is a best set of moral rules, I have serious doubts. That is, I do not doubt that some moralities are better than others— only that there is such a thing as the best morality.

At any rate, I have already adopted the spirit of relativism in an earlier chapter, and I see no reason to change here. Whether or not there is a best morality, we must make our decisions and judgments here and now.

THE REVERSAL I HAVE SUGGESTED does, I think, accommodate Williams's challenge. It does not, of course, accommodate Nietzsche's. To do that, it would have to accommodate people who are not both decent and honorable—people whose principles are not acceptable to the society in which they live, who may show incomprehensible indifference or contempt toward their obligations or other people. And that, again, is further than the impersonal point of view can go.

But the force of Nietzsche's challenge is not thereby diminished. Such people can be perfectly rational, after all, and they can also live by a demanding personal moral code. What sets them apart is that they do not share society's perceptions in depth. They cannot incorporate impersonal morality into their own moral lives.

What, finally, can we say about such people? I'm not sure. Part of my problem is that I'm not sure how many there really are. People can easily enough claim to be following a personal morality when they are merely pursuing their own self-interest. And even if they are pursuing personal conceptions of the good, their rejection of shared conceptions may not be rationally justified. Certainly, the photographer's rejection does not seem to be. It is very difficult to imagine that careful deliberation and reflection could have led him to the conclusion that what he did was the best thing for him to do. And if it could have, we would have great difficulty not thinking him demented.

Whether such a person must really be demented I cannot say. Indeed, I'm not even sure what force the 'really' has here. What I do know is that when someone's perceptions are so unlike the perceptions of the rest of us, we cannot, psychologically, merely consider him a Nietzschean free spirit. He is too fundamentally unlike the rest of us.

Still, to conclude that any Nietzschean free spirit must be demented is to embrace what I take to be unacceptable externalist assumptions. Plausible candidates for free spirits who are not demented include various artists who reject society's perceptions in ways we have less trouble making sense of—the young Henry Miller in Paris, say, or the real Gauguin, as opposed to the one imagined by Williams. We can make sense of their individual pursuits of their own good lives—perhaps even envy or admire them for it—because their lives are deeply tied to impulses we can recognize in ourselves.

A decent and honorable man would not, like Miller, sponge off his friends while seducing their wives and then write about it in deliberately obscene prose, but even those of us who are decent and honorable can recognize that Miller is not *fundamentally* unlike us. We can understand a good life built around moral and literary experimentation, and we can understand how, in the case of Miller, the two can be intertwined. We can also understand how his pursuit of that good life could lead him to reject certain obligations that matter deeply to the rest of us. Had he rejected the obligations that the photographer rejected, however, our understanding would have ended. At that point he would have become fundamentally unlike us.

Since he was not, many of us have no trouble saying about him what we cannot say about the photographer. Some might say, for instance, that he was a moral man whose personal morality we cannot accept. Others might say that people like Miller should not be judged according to conventional moral standards but according to the standards they choose to live by. Still others might say that to ask people like Miller to share society's perceptions in depth is to ask too much of them.

However we choose to put it, the point is this: People like Miller personify Nietzsche's challenge. They live according to their own conceptions of the good, not our shared conception of the good. From the impersonal point of view, they are not moral. They reject many of society's rules. But by their own lights they are.

The same can be said of G. Gordon Liddy, whose personal moral code is far more demanding than our own shared morality. The principles that guided his behavior during Watergate and its aftermath set him apart from us—more so, perhaps, than Miller, but certainly less so than the photographer. Although many people consider him something of a fruitcake, that judgment is not psychologically forced on us. He does not seem to be fundamentally unlike us.

The notion of someone being fundamentally unlike us is not a very sharp one. Its ambit is defined only by our psychological capacities. It sets apart those we cannot help but consider moral monsters from those we can see as unlike us but connected to us just the same. If it is capable of doing real moral work, it can soften what is most disturbing about Nietzsche's challenge. Whether it is so capable I don't yet know.

7

TRUISMS REVISITED

IN THE FIRST CHAPTER, I set myself two tasks. The first was to see how strongly a moral theory could accommodate three truisms. The second was to answer a question I took to be at the heart of ethics.

The truisms were these: First, moral rules are society's rules. Second, morality is a matter of individual choice. Third, some things are wrong regardless of what any society or individual has to say about them. And the question was this: Does anybody or anything have any moral authority over how I am to lead *my* life?

It's now time to see how I've done.

THE TRUISMS SEEM to have fared well. Indeed, they seem to have survived in their strongest forms.

Consider the first. Moral rules are, I have maintained throughout, society's rules. They are mutually agreed upon rules intended to provide reasons for acting for all members of society. That puts me in agreement with such neo-Kantian contractarians as Baier. I have also maintained throughout that the course of action dictated by these rules—the best course of action according to the reasons they provide—is what one ought to do. That also puts me in agreement with Baier and the others.

Other things I have maintained put me in decided disagreement. For one, I have denied that moral rules encompass all there is to morality. To ask what one ought to do is not to take *the* moral point of view, but *one* moral point of view—the impersonal one. The other, of course, is the personal one. To take *that* moral point of view is to ask a very different question: What's the best thing for *me* to do according to my own moral commitments—my conception of the good, my ground projects, my personal ideals and principles.

For most of us, our moral commitments include our obligations to others according to society's rules. The strength of our commitment varies—from person to person and from obligation to obligation. These variations might be due to unprincipled self-interest, but they might also be due to other, stronger moral commitments.

And that brings me to another fundamental disagreement with neo-Kantians (and, for the matter, unprefixed Kantians). The impersonal point of view neither rationally nor morally overrides the personal one. In other words, morality is a matter of personal choice. And that is the second truism.

To say that the impersonal point of view does not rationally override the personal is to make a point about practical reason, not about morality. Even an unprincipled egoist can be rational. Whether any reason for acting—including any reason provided by moral rules—is some individual's reason for acting, or whether that reason rationally overrides some other reason for acting, depends on that individual's motivation set.

To say that the impersonal point of view does not morally override the personal *is* to make a point about morality. The unprincipled egoist may be rational, but he is hardly moral. He has a personal point of view, but not a moral one. The rest of us do. And whether the reasons provided by moral rules override our other moral commitments is morally, as well as rationally, up to us. If careful deliberation and reflection lead me to the conclusion that my other moral commitments take precedence, I am no less moral for it. That is the force of the second truism.

What about the third truism? Are some things wrong regardless of what any society or individual has to say? Yes. Does that weaken the first two truisms? No. Here's why.

For one thing, even though moral rules are society's rules, not all of society's rules are valid. To be valid, they must be freely chosen by the members of that society. If they are not, they do not create real mutually agreed upon rights. The moral rules permitting segregation during the Jim Crow period in the American south, for example, were not freely chosen by blacks. So they were not valid rules. Blacks had no moral obligation to acquiesce to them, and whites had no mutually agreed upon right to demand that they acquiesce—regardless of society's rules permitting segregation.

Of course, rules permitting segregation might be valid in some other society, as long as people of both races freely choose them. If, however, there are practices that no valid rules could permit, these practices are wrong regardless of what any society has to say.

In saying that there are Kantian constraints on moral rules I am again in agreement with the neo-Kantians. Such constraints are built into the impersonal point of view. They don't weaken the first truism—moral rules remain society's rules—but they do distinguish rules that—from the impersonal point of view—make real claims on individuals from those that do not.

These constraints are not, however, built into the personal point of view. So even if some act is wrong from the impersonal point of view, even, that is, if one ought not do it, it may still be justified from the personal point of view.

That is why the third truism (any more than the first) does not dilute the second. Right and wrong—what one ought and ought not do—are determined from the impersonal point of view. The personal point of view determines only the best thing for some individual to do. It may override the impersonal, but it does not change it. So some things may be wrong regardless of what any individual has to say.

WHAT ABOUT THE ANSWER to the question? *Does* anybody or anything have any moral authority over how I lead my life? The answer seems to be no, given the survival of the second truism in its strongest form.

When I posed the question at the close of the first chapter, I was not at all certain what the answer would be. As the eventual answer became clearer to me, I anticipated it with mixed feelings. On the one hand, there seemed something profoundly right about it, independent of philosophical argument. Nietzschean autonomy, the autonomy to live my good life as I see it, to pursue my ground projects, to live according to my own principles, is much more precious than Kantian autonomy, the autonomy to subject myself to the impersonal point of view.

But there also seemed something profoundly disturbing about it. If Nietzschean autonomy is more precious, it is not yet enough. To say that the full moral life does not require us to respect our obligations to others is to say something much stronger than what seems profoundly right about Nietzsche. Hence, my mixed feelings.

Hence, also, my division of the question of moral freedom into two challenges—Nietzsche's and Williams's. About the latter I had no mixed feelings. Even if it could be met, which I am now certain it cannot, a morality that accommodates it is better than one that meets it. Any morality that requires decent and honorable people always to do what one ought to do requires too much of them. That is Williams's challenge and there is nothing disturbing about it. Whether my own way of accommodating it proves disturbing remains to be seen.

BUT MY ANSWER TO THE QUESTION of moral freedom went further than that, all the way to Nietzschean freedom. And I want to close this book with some final reflections on that.

Not too long ago, an assertion of the strongest version of the second truism would have surprised nobody. In the heyday of emotivism, prescriptivism, and any other form of noncognitivism that might have been advanced during the period when analytic philosophy was in ascendance, individual moral freedom was taken as a matter of course by most philosophers in the English speaking world.

We have, to be sure, come a long way since then. Investigations into social contract theory, practical reason, and semantics have changed our way of looking at morality. And the results of these investigations have, for the most part, been welcome. Not only is it liberating to be rid of the task of asking ourselves over and over again what the word "good" means, or what speech act it is characteristically used to perform, but we have gained a deeper understanding of moral rules and moral reasoning. For taking us back to real ethics, the neo-Kantians deserve real credit and thanks.

But something has been lost in the return. If the noncognitivists lost sight of the first and third truisms, at least they had a firm hold on the second. If they were blind to even the possibility that there are moral truths from the impersonal point of view, they were not blind to something of equal importance. People are valuing beings. Some of their values are highly personal, and some of their personal values are moral values. And that's what has been lost, or, at the very least, been given very short shrift.

The personal moral point of view, in short, has been driven out by the impersonal. Certainly, Williams has done much to bring it back, and for that *he* deserves real credit and thanks. So, for that matter, does Nagel, for recognizing the force of Williams's challenge and realizing that it must be accommodated.

But Williams's challenge leads directly to Nietzsche's. And that leads directly to what the noncognitivists seem to have been right about. Put in a way they would no doubt have rejected: Regardless of what moral truths there may be from the impersonal point of view, human beings live their lives from the personal. Even if they ask themselves what one ought to do, the decision to do what one ought to do is not, as Baier would have it, merely an executive task, but a task of practical reason, carried out in accordance with their own moral commitments. And however their commitments may differ from ours, they may very well be reasoning and deciding morally.

THAT'S THE FIRST REFLECTION. The second is this. Williams has wondered why it is so important to some moral philosophers that they be able to call egoists irrational.[1] Isn't it enough that we can call them selfish, cruel, unfair, and any number of other things? Can we ever hope to dissuade a burglar by reading (or explaining) Kant or Baier to him?

Similar thoughts are appropriate in light of the force of Nietzsche's challenge. Suppose we are forced to admit that the photographer acted rationally and according to his own moral commitments. If what I've been saying is right, we must also say that he reasoned and decided morally. But that does not stop us from calling him cruel and monstrous. Nor does it stop us from calling what he did heinous and abominable (or, more important for our own safety, from putting him in prison for the rest of his life).

These thick moral concepts, as Williams calls them, do express a kind of moral knowledge.[2] If the knowledge that they apply to him and what he did was not enough to dissuade him from doing it, what could we gain by adding that he didn't act according to moral rules and there's no more to morality than that?

One thing, I suppose, is a kind of moral coherence. But that kind of coherence, like that proposed by MacIntyre, comes at too great a cost—the loss of the personal moral point of view. Besides, I don't think that our failure to add such an ineffective (and untrue) claim reveals any lack of moral coherence. If it does, this book has been seriously misguided.

Another, I suppose, is a certain peace of mind. "Relativism," like "reductionism," has become something of a buzz word of late. Witness, in this regard, the stunning popularity of Allan Bloom's polemic against creeping (or should I say "rampant"?) Nietzschean-ism and our preoccupation with personal values.[3] But that peace of mind can be gained in other ways. Nothing I've said in this book stops us from teaching and defending the reasonableness of our moral rules to our children and students, nor does it stop us from teaching or defending our shared conceptions of the good, nor does it stop us from trying to develop in them the dispositions and principles of decent and honorable people.

THAT'S MY SECOND REFLECTION. Here's my third and final reflection.

After reading a couple of the foregoing chapters, James Sterba asked me whether it is a consequence of my views on practical reason that the photographer could have acted in perfect accord with reason. Despite the externalist phrasing of the question, I pondered it seriously. Did I really think that the photographer could have acted rationally?

The photographer's story was originally introduced to provide an example of something wrong regardless of what any society or individual had to say about it. It became, in the end, the strongest test of Nietzsche's challenge. And I am obviously uncomfortable about it in a way I am obviously not uncomfortable about people like Miller and Liddy.

My pondering of Sterba's question led me to realize how deeply uncomfortable I was. It also led me to make the distinctions in the previous chapter between those who are fundamentally unlike us and those who are not, and between what we are psychologically able to accept and what we are not, and between those we are psychologically forced to consider demented and those we are not. I concluded that chapter with the confession that I did not know whether such distinctions can do any moral work. I still don't.

One reason to think they might is this: Let's suppose, again, that the photographer made his decision after careful reflection on his motivation set and that his decision was fully in keeping with his own conception of the good. What we seem to be faced with is a colossal failure of socialization, so colossal that it cries out for explanation. The kind of explanation we expect is a psychological one, much like the one offered by Meyer Levin in *Compulsion*, his fictionalized account of the Leopold-Loeb case. And when we get it, we are relieved. The photographer and the kidnapper-killers are sick.

The problem, though, is that psychological explanations are equally available for Jonas Salk, Saul Bellow, Julius Erving, or any of us.

What separates the photographer from the rest of us, then, is not the availability of psychological explanation, but what is to be explained—that he turned out so fundamentally unlike the rest of us that we are psychologically unable to think of him as fully rational.

Put another way, we, like any society, have our normal types. Salk, Bellow and Erving distinguish themselves by their remarkable accomplishments. They are like us but exemplary. Liddy distinguishes himself by being at the fringe of our normal types. He is unlike us, but in a comprehensible way. The photographer distinguishes himself by being thoroughly abnormal. There are fundamental moral and psychological differences between him and the rest of us, but that, of itself, is not enough to give our judgment that he *must* be demented the weight it needs to do real moral work.

What would be enough? One possibility is a convincing argument that some desires are intrinsically irrational. Parfit has suggested (but not argued for) one such candidate—the desire to jump that many of us feel when atop a high precipice. He has also suggested (and argued for) another—any pattern of concern that makes purely arbitrary distinctions, such as a concern for everyone within exactly one mile of me and no concern for anyone beyond exactly one mile.[4] Perhaps he is right about those, but they do not seem to apply to the photographer. If a convincing argument about other desires is forthcoming, and if it can be applied to the photographer, then my discomfort will be assuaged. Unfortunately, I don't have one.

No doubt there are many other possibilities, but as long as they remain just possibilities I'll leave off listing them. I'd rather end on a more positive note.

To question whether the distinctions I've been discussing can do real moral work is to question from a decidedly theoretical perspective. In terms of our ordinary moral lives, they are of enormous importance, and that importance I do not question. If the photographer appalls us in a way that Miller does not, it is for good reasons. They may not be the photographer's reasons, but that doesn't make them any the worse.

NOTES

Chapter 1

1. This answer runs through most of Baier's work—including most notably ch. 12 of Kurt Baier, *The Moral Point of View* (Ithaca, N.Y.: Cornell University Press, 1958).

2. Bernard Williams, "Internal and External Reasons," in *Moral Luck* (Cambridge, Eng.: Cambridge University Press, 1981), pp. 101–13.

3. Hence Baier's contrast between morality and the Sierra Club in Kurt Baier, "Moral Reasons," in *Midwest Studies in Philosophy*, Vol. III (Minneapolis: University of Minnesota Press, 1980), pp. 62–74.

4. Gilbert Harman, *The Nature of Morality* (New York: Oxford University Press, 1977), p. 59.

5. For a brief overview, see J. Baird Callicott's "Non-anthropocentric Value Theory and Environmental Ethics," *American Philosophical Quarterly* 21 (1984): 299–309.

6. Arthur Schopenhauer, *On the Basis of Morality* trans. E. F. J. Payne, (Indianapolis: Bobbs-Merrill, 1965), p. 96.

Chapter 2

1. For Hare, see R. M. Hare, *The Language of Morals* (New York: Oxford University Press, 1952). For Harman, see Gilbert Harman, *The Nature of Morality* (New York: Oxford University Press, 1977), p. 151.

2. Bernard Williams, "Persons, Character and Morality," in *Moral Luck* (Cambridge, Eng.: Cambridge University Press, 1981), pp. 1–19.

3. *Ibid.* See also the title essay of the same volume.

4. Bernard Williams, *Ethics and the Limits of Philosophy* (Cambridge, Mass.: Harvard University Press, 1985). See especially the first chapter.

5. Kurt Baier, *The Moral Point of View* (Ithaca, N.Y.: Cornell University Press, 1981).

6. See, for example, Kurt Baier, "Moral Reasons," in *Midwest Studies in Philosophy*, Vol. III (Minneapolis: University of Minnesota Press, 1980), pp. 63–74.

Chapter 3

1. Gilbert Harman, "Practical Reasoning," *Review of Metaphysics* 29 (1975–76). For his views on epistemic reasoning, see Gilbert Harman, *Thought* (Princeton, N.J.: Princeton University Press, 1973).

2. In Kurt Baier, "The Social Source of Reason," Baier's 1977 Presidential Address to the APA Eastern Division Meeting, which appeared in *Proceedings and Addresses of the American Philosophical Association* 51 (1978): 707–33.

3. Bernard Williams, "Internal and External Reasons," in *Moral Luck* (Cambridge, Eng.: Cambridge University Press, 1981), pp. 101–13.

4. See both Gilbert Harman, *The Nature of Morality*, (New York: Oxford University Press, 1977), ch. 9, and Harman, "Relativistic Ethics: Morality as Politics," in *Midwest Studies in Philosophy*, Vol. III (Minneapolis: University of Minnesota Press, 1980), pp. 109–21.

5. Bernard Williams, "Moral Luck," in *Moral Luck*.

6. Bernard Williams, "Persons, Character and Morality," in *Moral Luck*, p. 18.

7. Nietzsche's challenge to morality also runs through much of his work. The formulation I draw from here comes from sec. 106, Bk. II, of Friedrich Nietzsche, *Daybreak,* trans. R. J. Hollingdale. (Cambridge, Eng.: Cambridge University Press, 1982).

Chapter 4

1. Daniel Dennett, "Intentional Systems," in *Brainstorms* (Cambridge, Mass.: Bradford Books, 1978).

2. In Bernard Williams, *Ethics and the Limits of Philosophy* (Cambridge, Mass.: Harvard University Press, 1985), pp. 62–63.

3. This point, like others of Sartre's I note below, is from Jean Paul Sartre, *Being and Nothingness*, trans. Hazel E. Barnes (New York: Citadel Press, 1965).

4. Otto Neurath, "Protocol Sentences," first published in *Erkenntis* 3 (1932–33) and available in *Logical Positivism*, ed. A. J. Ayer (New York: Free Press, 1959), pp. 199–208.

5. Stephen Darwall, *Impartial Reason* (Ithaca and London: Cornell University Press, 1983).

6. Paul Taylor, "On Taking the Moral Point of View," *Midwest Studies in Philosophy*, Vol. III (Minneapolis: University of Minnesota Press, 1980), pp. 35–61.

Chapter 5

1. In chapter 7 of John Rawls, *A Theory of Justice* (Cambridge, Mass.: Harvard University Press, 1971).

2. In Bernard Williams, "Moral Luck," in *Moral Luck* (Cambridge, Eng.: Cambridge University Press, 1981). In "Persons, Character and Morality," alsoin *Moral Luck*, he makes a similar point, using the phrase *from now*.

3. In Alisdair MacIntyre, *After Virtue* (Notre Dame, Ind.: University of Notre Dame Press, 1984).

4. Alisdair MacIntyre, "The Magic in the Pronoun 'My,'" *Ethics* 94 (1983): 113–25.

5. The passage, which MacIntyre quotes on pp. 257–58 of *After Virtue*, is from note 962 of *The Will to Power*.

6. Bernard Williams, *Ethics and the Limits of Philosophy* (Cambridge, Mass.: Harvard University Press, 1985), p. 202.

7. His comments on both Marx and St. Benedict are in the final chapter of *After Virtue*.

8. Rawls, *Theory of Justice*, esp. secs. 66–68.

9. Thomas Nagel, *The View from Nowhere* (Oxford and New York: Oxford University Press, 1986), ch. 10, "Living Right and Living Well."

10. See note 5.

11. Williams, "Persons, Character and Morality."

12. Hilary Putnam, *Reason, Truth and History* (Cambridge, Eng.: Cambridge University Press, 1981), pp. 171–73.

Chapter 6

1. Philippa Foot, "Morality as a System of Hypothetical Imperatives," reprinted in George Sher (ed.), *Moral Philosophy* (San Diego and New York: Harcourt, Brace, Jovanovich, 1987), pp. 293–301.

2. Susan Woff, "Moral Saints," *Journal of Philosophy* 79 (1982): 419–39.

3. Marcia Baron, "The Alleged Moral Repugnance of Acting from Duty," *Journal of Philosophy* 81 (1984): 197–220. Both Baron's and Wolf's papers are reprinted in Sher (ed.), *Moral Philosophy*.

4. See "The Concluding Chapter" of Derek Parfit, *Reasons and Persons* (Oxford and New York: Oxford University Press, 1986).

5. Wolf, "Moral Saints."

Chapter 7

1. Bernard Williams, *Ethics and the Limits of Philosophy* (Cambridge, Mass.: Harvard University Press, 1985), pp. 23–24.

2. *Ibid.*, esp. chs. 7–9.

3. Allan Bloom, *The Closing of the American Mind* (New York: Simon and Schuster, 1987).

4. Derek Parfit, *Reasons and Persons* (Oxford and New York: Oxford University Press, 1986), sec. 46. I should note that Parfit doesn't say that all desires to jump are irrational, but only that some *might* be.

INDEX

A

Apartment, The, 112
Aristotle, 11, 12, 45, 63, 93, 95; on the good
    life, 81, 86, 89, 101, 102
Atwell, John, 84

B

Baier, Kurt, 5, 9, 11, 28, 30, 95, 124, 131, 136;
    on practical reason, 33, 35, 41, 45–49, 54,
    70
Baron, Marcia, 112
Benedict, Saint, 94
Berkeley, George, 40, 44
Bloom, Allan, 137
Bohr, Niels, 44

C

Chomsky, Noam, 44

D

Darwall, Stephen, 69–72, 74
Dennett, Daniel, 62–63

E

Egoism, 22, 49, 51, 54–56, 132
Einstein, Albert, 44

Index

Index

R

Rawls, John, 48, 95; Aristotelian principle of, 99–101, 104; on moral goodness, 105–6; on rational life plans, 85–89, 99
Relativism, 55, 127–28, 137
Ross, David, 60, 117

S

Sartre, Jean-Paul, 68, 71
Schopenhauer, Arthur, 17
Skinner, B. F., 44
Sterba, James, 137–38

T

Taylor, Paul, 74–76
Two for the Road, 102–4

U

Utilitarianism, 17, 61, 117

V

Virtues, 83, 91, 93, 105–7, 121, 123

W

Wilder, Billy, 112
Williams, Bernard, 29–30, 65, 86, 92–94, 96,